E. M. Forster

Revised Edition

Twayne's English Authors Series

Kinley E. Roby, *Editor*
Northeastern University

TEAS 89

E. M. FORSTER
(1879–1970)
Courtesy of King's College Library,
King's College, Cambridge University

E. M. Forster

Revised Edition

By Frederick P. W. McDowell

University of Iowa

Twayne Publishers · Boston

E. M. Forster, Revised Edition

Frederick P. W. McDowell

Revised Edition copyright © 1982
Twayne Publishers
A Division of G. K. Hall & Company
70 Lincoln Street
Boston, Massachusetts 02111

Printed on permanent/durable acid-
free paper and bound in The United
States of America.

Library of Congress Cataloging in Publication Data

McDowell, Frederick P. W.
E. M. Forster.

(Twayne's English authors series ; TEAS 89)
Bibliography: p. 160
Includes index.
1. Forster, E. M. (Edward Morgan), 1879–1970—
Criticism and interpretation.   I. Title.   II. Series
PR6011.058Z822 1982   823′.912   81–6735
ISBN 0–8057–6817–3   AACR2

Contents

About the Author

Frederick P. W. McDowell is Professor of English at the University of Iowa, where he has taught since 1949. He received the B. S. and M. A. degrees from the University of Pennsylvania and the M. A. and Ph.D. degrees from Harvard University. He began teaching at Washington and Jefferson College and the University of Delaware prior to serving in the United States Army from 1941 to 1946.

A specialist in British and American literature after 1850, Professor McDowell is widely known as a Forster scholar. He wrote the first edition of *E. M. Forster* (1969) for the Twayne English Authors Series and has written numerous essays and essay-reviews on Forster. He is the editor of the authoritative *E. M. Forster: An Annotated Bibliography of Secondary Writings about Him* (Northern Illinois University Press, 1977), which covers writings on Forster for seventy years. He abstracted all of the items except for some in foreign languages.

Other books by Professor McDowell include volumes on Ellen Glasgow, Elizabeth Madox Roberts, and Caroline Gordon; and he has published articles on such writers as Thomas Hardy, Joseph Conrad, Virginia Woolf, W. H. Auden, Robert Penn Warren, and Angus Wilson. He has also written extensively on Bernard Shaw, and has a reputation as an expert on Shaw.

Preface

Why is a revised edition of *E. M. Forster* necessary? Why could not the first edition of 1969 be reprinted to satisfy the continuing demand for an overview of Forster?

In the first place, there is Forster's reputation. In 1967–68 Forster was still alive and had consolidated for himself a position as an outstanding English novelist. His high reputation resulted not only from the worth of the writings and from the number of excellent critical studies done on him beginning with Lionel Trilling's *E. M. Forster* (1943) and James McConkey's *The Novels of E. M. Forster* (1957), but it also derived from his continuing presence as grand old man of letters and sage at King's College, Cambridge University. My earlier Twayne book could be regarded as one of the final contributions to the consolidation of Forster's reputation before his death.

The burden of the numerous critical studies from Trilling's in 1943 to my own in 1969 was that the novels were preeminent, but that the nonfiction writings, if less arresting, were also significant and in some respects unique. With *A Passage to India* (1924) Forster's early reputation reached its zenith, with a kind of afterglow provided by *Aspects of the Novel* (1927). Forster ceased to publish fiction after 1924 but he attained a respected position as polemicist in the cause of liberalism, especially after it was threatened by Nazi totalitarianism and by more subtle forms of repression on the British scene. In the 1940s, as a result of the war and of the work of Trilling and others, Forster came into his own as an important, and conceivably great, writer and intellectual influence. With the publication of McConkey's study in 1957, a flood of books and articles supervened, and Forster's reputation with critics, literary historians, and the reading public was secure. His physical presence signified that a great artist from the past had survived to be in our midst, an artist who was also a formidable, forceful, and original intellectual presence.

When Forster died in 1970, there were signs that his preeminence was about to be challenged. In some of the reviews of the authorized life by P. N. Furbank, the slimness rather than the originality of the achievement was emphasized and the relevance of the early novels for people living in later years of the century was sometimes in question. The inevitable reaction took place that occurs after a writer's death; and as Forster became less popular with the intelligentsia, the achievement of his rival, Virginia Woolf, began to loom larger. Whatever the final merit of his work in comparison with that of his contemporaries, the fiction still retains its freshness and complexity, and the nonfiction still compels our attention by virtue of its originality and our consciousness that Forster was both an honest and charismatic writer.

Coupled with this more or less expected revaluation of the work after Forster's death was the response to the publication of Forster's homosexual novel, *Maurice*, and to the short stories on homosexual themes (*The Life to Come and Other Stories*, 1972). Reactions to these works engendered controversy, and those who felt that the posthumous works were weak tended to see them as typical of an attenuated achievement. Some element of shock was involved; and for most readers the disclosure of Forster's homosexuality entailed some adjustment in their views of him. It gave us, if nothing else, another lens through which to see him. Furbank's candid and honest *E. M. Forster: A Life* (1977 and 1978) allowed us to see that the saintly sage at Cambridge, England, was only one of the masks that Forster used to cover a warm sensual temperament which tried in various ways to find emotional, physical, and spiritual fulfillment.

Do the revelations in the posthumous writings and in Furbank's biography compel us to judge the novels and the other works differently? Yes, insofar as we can see added implications to many of the relationships charted in them: those between Gino Carella and Philip Herriton in *Where Angels Fear to Tread*, or between Rickie Elliott and Stewart Ansell or between Rickie and Stephen Wonham in *The Longest Journey*, or between Aziz and Fielding in *A Passage to India*. And we can interpret in a more specific way than formerly Forster's famous statement in "What I Believe," that he would prefer to betray his country rather than his friend. But we get, at best, only another dimension for these works, which is by no means the sole dimension found in them. We see the works differently as a result of what we now know; but, paradoxically, we see them, too, as they always were.

The added information that we now have on other aspects of Forster's career and personality besides the sexual is indispensable in seeing Forster as he really was. As a result of the biography, we know more fully Forster's involvement with his female relatives and his rebellion in the 1930s against their influence; we see more clearly the extent of the Alexandrian and the Indian experiences; and we realize that Forster's involvement with liberal causes, especially during "the low, dishonest decade" of the 1930s and after, was not merely superficial. And appropriately with a writer for whom personal relations were so important, we learn more than we knew previously of Forster's friends and acquaintances, literary and otherwise—for example, Joe Ackerley, Syed Ross Masood, and Bob Buckingham. We see him now as a man among his contemporaries rather than as an Olympian sage.

I have reorganized my first chapter to make it less a summary of Forster's attitudes and a calendar of his beliefs than a summary of his career, but a summary seen in relationship to what he wrote. I discuss more briefly the leading characteristics of his mind in my first chapter or let them emerge at other points in my study. I have become even more convinced than I was in 1968 that Forster is a "symbolist" and a "romancer" or nothing, and I have interpreted the fiction more fully in that direction. I have revised extensively the discussions of the early novels. Having lived with them for so long, I now regard *A Room with a View*, for example, as a masterpiece, and *The Longest Journey* as undiminished in its charm, appeal, and freshness. I have, moreover, included a discussion of *Maurice* and the other posthumously published fiction, most of it in short story form. I have given in the critiques of the individual novels some materials as to the genesis of each work, since these facts are now more completely known than they were fifteen years ago. Except to add background information, I have changed very little my presentation of *A Passage to India*. Later criticism has amplified rather than changed my views on Forster's greatest work.

The hold that Forster exerted over his contemporaries when he was alive has diminished, and he has had to sacrifice whatever in his reputation may have been unsound. But his works still stand as revelations of a deeply penetrating sensibility and of a mind remarkable for its durable insights. If anything, his fascination as man and writer has been augmented, even though his authority may have lessened.

Frederick P. W. McDowell

University of Iowa

Acknowledgments

I am indebted to Professor Richard Lloyd-Jones, who, as chairman of the Department of English at the University of Iowa, has supported me as a colleague over the years. I am also grateful to the Graduate College of the University of Iowa for providing me with funds for typing and for financial assistance which enabled me to participate in 1979 in the Centenary Conference on Forster at Concordia University, Montreal, and in a Centenary Seminar on Forster at the Modern Language Association convention. Forsterians in Europe, Canada, India, Australia, and the United States have assisted me with their expertise and friendship: J. B. Beer, John Colmer, G. K. Das, Joseph Dobrinsky, Peter Firchow, P. N. Furbank, Philip Gardner, Elizabeth Heine, Judith S. Herz, James McConkey, S. P. Rosenbaum, V. A. Shahane, Wilfred Stone, George H. Thomson, Alan Wilde, and the late Oliver Stallybrass. Professors Dobrinsky and Thomson read my manuscript and offered valuable suggestions. My wife, Margaret, has helped by her patience and interest.

Acknowledgment is made to these organizations for permission to reprint from E. M. Forster's works:

Edward Arnold, Ltd. for *Where Angels Fear to Tread, A Room with a View, The Longest Journey, Howards End, A Passage to India, Aspects of the Novel, Goldsworthy Lowes Dickinson, Abinger Harvest, Two Cheers for Democracy, The Hill of Devi, Maurice, The Life to Come and Other Stories,* and *Arctic Summer and Other Fiction;*

King's College, Cambridge and The Society of Authors as the literary representative of the E. M. Forster estate for *Pharos and Pharillon;*

Doubleday, Page and Co. for *Alexandria: A History and a Guide;*

Oxford University Press for "Introduction" to *The Longest Journey,* World's Classics;

Harcourt, Brace, Jovanovich, Inc. for *A Passage to India,*

E. M. FORSTER

Aspects of the Novel, Goldsworthy Lowes Dickinson, Abinger Harvest, Two Cheers for Democracy, and *The Hill of Devi;*
Alfred A. Knopf, Inc. for *Where Angels Fear to Tread, The Longest Journey, A Room with a View,* and *Howards End;*
W. W. Norton and Co., Inc. for *Maurice* and *The Life to Come and Other Short Stories.*
The photograph opposite the title page is reproduced through courtesy of King's College Library, Cambridge University.
For permission to quote from my previously published essays, I acknowledge the cooperation of the editors of *PMLA (Howards End), Critique (The Longest Journey), Modern Fiction Studies* (the short stories), and *Virginia Woolf Quarterly* (*Maurice* and the later short stories).

Chronology

1910	*Howards End*, London and New York. Achieved wide recognition. *Arctic Summer* begun; abandoned, 1912.
1911	*The Celestial Omnibus and Other Stories. A Room with a View* published in America.
1912–1913	October–March: first visit to India. Visited Masood, Maharajah of Chhatarpur, and Maharajah of Dewas State Senior.
1913	Began *A Passage to India*. Visited Edward Carpenter at Millthorpe; contact with George Merrill caused Forster to acknowledge his homosexuality. Began *Maurice*.
1914	Completed *Maurice* in first form. Wrote essays and reviews for *New Weekly*. Became cataloger at National Gallery.
1915	Brief friendship with D. H. Lawrence. November 1915 to January 1919: volunteer officer, as "searcher," with Red Cross in Alexandria. Met C. P. Cavafy and later publicized his work.
1916	Meeting with Mohammed el Adl; they became intimate, 1917.
1919	Returned to England; wrote for *Nation, Athenaeum*, etc.
1920	Literary editor of *Daily Herald. Where Angels Fear to Tread* published in America. *The Story of the Siren*.
1921	March–October: second visit to India, as private secretary to Maharajah of Dewas State Senior. Visited Masood. *Howards End* reissued in America. Further work on *A Passage to India*.
1922	Left India, January. *Alexandria: A History and a Guide*, Alexandria. *The Longest Journey* published in America. Death of Mohammed el Adl. Met J. R. Ackerley who became close friend.
1923	*Pharos and Pharillon*, Richmond and New York. *A Room with a View* reissued in America. *The Celestial Omnibus* published in America.
1924	*A Passage to India* received with almost unanimous praise, England and America. First signifi-

cant meeting with T. E. Lawrence. Novels reissued, London. Mother inherited use of West Hackhurst (designed by Forster's father), Abinger Hammer, Surrey. Moved there from Weybridge.

1925   Received Femina Vie Heureuse and James Tait Black Memorial Prizes for *A Passage to India*.

1926   Affair with Harry Daley, London policeman, until about 1929.

1927   Delivered Clark Lectures, Trinity College, Cambridge: published as *Aspects of the Novel*, London and New York.

1928   *The Eternal Moment and Other Stories*, London and New York.

1930   Met Bob Buckingham, London policeman, who became closest friend. Defended D. H. Lawrence against T. S. Eliot.

1932   Met Christopher Isherwood. Marriage of Buckingham.

1934   *Goldsworthy Lowes Dickinson*, London and New York. President of National Council for Civil Liberties, 1934–1935; again President, 1942; resigned, 1948. "The Abinger Pageant" produced at Abinger Hammer in collaboration with Ralph Vaughan Williams. Wrote "Notes on the Way," 1934–1935, for *Time and Tide*.

1935   Addressed International Congress of Writers, Paris, on "Liberty in England."

1936   *Abinger Harvest*, London and New York.

1937   Death of Masood and Maharajah of Dewas State Senior.

1938   "England's Pleasant Land," pageant produced in collaboration with Ralph Vaughan Williams. Contributed to *Nation* (N.Y.) series, "Living Philosophies"; essay became in revised form, "What I Believe."

1940   *Nordic Twilight*.

1941   *Virginia Woolf: The Rede Lecture*. Began broadcasting to India for BBC. Protested effectively censorship of BBC.

1943	Lionel Trilling's *E. M. Forster* and republishing of novels in America inaugurated "Forster Revival."
1944	Presided at P. E. N. Conference to celebrate tercentenary of Milton's *Areopagitica*. Trilling's book published, London.
1945	*The Development of English Prose between 1918 and 1939* (The Ker Lecture). October–December: third visit to India, to attend P. E. N. Conference at Jaipur. Mother died; vacated West Hackhurst. Became Honorary Fellow, King's College, Cambridge University, and permanent resident there.
1947	Visit to United States: address to "The Symposium on Music Criticism" at Harvard University, May 1–3, on "The *Raison d'Etre* of Criticism in the Arts." Uniform Pocket Edition of novels published. *The Collected Tales of E. M. Forster*, New York; as *The Collected Short Stories of E. M. Forster*, London, 1948.
1949	Second visit to United States: address to American Academy of Arts and Letters, on "Art for Art's Sake," May 27.
1951	*Two Cheers for Democracy*, London and New York.
1952	*Billy Budd*, London and New York (opera libretto, adapted with Eric Crozier from Herman Melville for Benjamin Britten).
1953	Award, Companion of Honor; received by Queen Elizabeth II, February 13. *The Hill of Devi*, London and New York.
1956	*Marianne Thornton: A Domestic Biography, 1797–1887*, London and New York.
1960	Dramatization of *A Passage to India* by Santha Rama Rau at Oxford; London run, April 20–December 3. Defense witness in trial of Lawrence's *Lady Chatterley's Lover*.
1961	*Alexandria*, New York. Named Companion of Literature by Royal Society of Literature, May 10.
1962	New York run, *A Passage to India*, January 31–May 10.

1964	Suffered first stroke.
1969	January 1: appointed to Order of Merit by Queen Elizabeth II.
1970	Death, June 7, at Coventry at home of the Buckinghams.
1971	*Maurice*, London and New York.
1972	*The Life to Come and Other Stories*, London; as *The Life to Come and Other Short Stories*, New York. London edition was first volume published of *The Abinger Edition of E. M. Forster*, under editorship of Oliver Stallybrass until his death, 1978.
1978	*Commonplace Book: E. M. Forster.*
1980	*Arctic Summer and Other Fiction.*

Chapter One
E. M. Forster: Life, Career, and Times

One "Who saw life steadily, and saw it whole": Forster in His Early Career

Now recognized as one of the great literary figures of the twentieth century, E. M. Forster was born in London on January 1, 1879, at 6 Melcombe Place, Dorset Square, London.[1] His paternal ancestors were the serious-minded Thorntons, while his maternal forebears were the more imaginative, easy-going Whichelos. Forster illustrated, in fact, both strands of the family heritage. His concern with ethical and metaphysical issues reflected the seriousness of the Thorntons who had had affiliations with the evangelical Clapham Sect of the early nineteenth century. In contrast, his capacity for enjoyment, his interest in art and music, his involvement with literature, and his basically dilettante disposition derived from his mother's family, though Alice Clara (Lily) Whichelo Forster did not always herself reveal much flexibility in her later years. Forster owed most to his aunt, Marianne Thornton, who died when he was eight, but who left him a legacy, in trust, of £8,000. As a result of her generosity, he could attend Cambridge University and then devote himself to writing rather than to making his way "in the great world" of commerce, the professions, and government service. Forster's father died a year and a half after his birth, and the boy had to rely upon his mother for nurture and guidance, a relationship that was both rewarding and inhibiting.

Of great importance to Forster was his residence with his mother at Rooksnest, a house in the country near Stevenage in Hertfordshire. He became the center of attention for admiring and protective female relatives, he was precocious intellectual-

1

ly and socially, and he became inbued with a transcendent, mystical feeling for nature at a time when the country was yet unspoiled, though the "creeping . . . red rust" of London, cited in the final pages of *Howards End*, even then was threatening the survival of rural England.

After attendance at a preparatory school in Eastbourne, Forster in adolescence became a dayboy at Tonbridge School. The family had meanwhile been forced to leave Rooksnest in 1903, and Forster and his mother resided now in Tonbridge. His experience at school was not a happy one, and he felt about it much as Rickie Elliot did about Sawston School in *The Longest Journey* when he first went there as teacher. Forster did not fit the prescriptive standards which the masters imposed on the students, nor did he seem to make any close friends.

A happier time was the matriculation at Cambridge University. King's College was, in Forster's view, all that Tonbridge School was not. Here the emphasis was on the arts and on liberal studies; here one could cultivate both personal relationships and intellectual expansiveness. Forster found his horizons enlarging as a result of the influence of such dons and fellows as J. E. M. McTaggart, a proponent of ethical idealism; Goldsworthy Lowes Dickinson, a charming person, an inspired teacher, and a minor man of letters; Nathaniel Wedd, an accomplished scholar in classics and greatly influential upon Forster; Oscar Browning, a colorful personality and professor of history; and, preeminently, G. E. Moore, who refuted the idealism of McTaggart and the Hegelians at Cambridge and who established the virtues in *Principia Ethica* (1903) of disinterested inquiry with respect to ethical principles. Forster's close friend of the period was H. O. Meredith, who helped make him conscious of his homosexual tendencies. Meredith was in part the prototype of the fervent and prophetic intellectual, Stewart Ansell, of *The Longest Journey*; and even more directly, he figured as the Clive Durham of *Maurice*. The attraction between Forster and Meredith was genuine, while Clive's intellectuality in *Maurice* is evidently a reflection of Meredith's. If the portrait of Clive is to be relied upon, the relationship between Forster and Meredith was mostly platonic, and physical expression of feeling was limited to romping and to cursory caresses.

Cambridge University meant for E. M. Forster a liberation of the spirit, a milieu in which the individual could thrive as an individual and develop his full capacities. The enthusiastic, almost reverential, attitude with which Forster regarded Cambridge he embodied in the early chapters of *The Longest Journey* and in his biography of Goldsworthy Lowes Dickinson. Powers in the individual which elsewhere split asunder seemed in Cambridge to fuse and unite. Cambridge, in short, showed him the way to the reconciling of extremes, the achieving of a vital middle way, the attainment of proportion as a dynamic ongoing process, aspirations also motivating Margaret Schlegel in *Howards End*. His own quest, then and later, was to seek that unity of which Dante, in Forster's view, dreamed in his conception of an earthly paradise. In defining his vision, Dante was able to discriminate "between the forces that make men alike and the forces that make men different—between the centripetal power that may lead to monotony, and the centrifugal power that may lead to war. These powers are reconciled in the orbits of the stars; and Dante's first and last word to us is that we should imitate the celestial harmony." [2]

Matthew Arnold spoke of such a necessity to develop the individual's latent gifts, and it comes as no surprise that Forster confessed indebtedness to Arnold's thought and temper.[3] Arnold might indeed have been speaking for E.M. Forster when he cited the powers that human nature must develop before a true culture can prevail: "the power of conduct . . . the power of intellect and knowledge, the power of beauty, the power of social life and manners." [4] Arnold was in large part instrumental in helping Forster define his point of view and his standards. These are some aspects of the Arnoldian heritage which found their way into Forster's philosophy and literary work: a reverence for culture as a spiritually renovating force, a revulsion from harsh and unimaginative bourgeois (or philistine) values, the need for men to test their beliefs and their powers in the marketplace as well as the ivory tower, the realization that "strictness of conscience" (Hebraism) and "spontaneity of consciousness" (Hellenism) are both respected human powers, the need for the individual to define his values by the exercise of the informed intelligence, the contrary realization that intelligence can take us only so far when intuition (or vision) must take over (Forster in *Goldsworthy Lowes Dickinson* speaks of both "the importance and the unimportance of reason"[5]), and the urgency for the truly perceptive individual to see life not only steadily but to see it whole (in *Howards End* Henry Wilcox seeks it steadily but Margaret Schlegel can also see it whole). Forster might have achieved substantially the same beliefs independently, since his humanism was temperamental as well as intellectual; but Arnold and Cambridge University helped him to define himself, to work out for himself a set of humanistic as opposed to sectarian religious values, and then to express them through the medium of literary art.

Through H. O. Meredith, who was not part of the later Bloomsbury circle, Forster became a member of the Cambridge Conversazione Society or the Apostles, a number of whom, including Forster himself, did form the nucleus for the later Bloomsbury coterie.[6] Among turn-of-the-century Apostles were Lytton Strachey, John Maynard Keynes, Leonard Woolf, Desmond MacCarthy, and Saxon Sydney-Turner; Roger Fry had been elected a member somewhat earlier. Another discussion group, "The Midnight Society," included Strachey, Woolf, Sydney-Turner, Thoby Stephen, and Clive Bell. These Cambridge men were nothing if not "advanced," and they found sustenance in such "radicals" as Henrik Ibsen, Bernard Shaw, Thomas Hardy, Samuel Butler, and Algernon Charles Swinburne.[7]

All of these Cambridge men, and Forster, were later active in the Bloomsbury circle in London as early as 1905; again about 1910–1911 and after; and then again with the founding of the Memoir Club, 1920. In London the group enlarged to include Virginia Stephen (Woolf), Vanessa Stephen (Bell), Adrian Stephen, Molly MacCarthy, and Duncan Grant. Most of these Bloomsbury figures later achieved fame: Strachey as critic, biographer, and historian; Leonard Woolf as political activist and theorist and as man of letters; Keynes as political and economics theorist; Fry and Clive Bell as art critics;

Desmond MacCarthy as drama critic; Grant and Vanessa Bell as painters; and Virginia Woolf as novelist. Thoby Stephen, who died from typhoid in 1906 after a trip to Greece, formed the link between his Cambridge friends and his sisters, Virginia and Vanessa.

Greatly influential on Bloomsbury were the dons and fellows in the Apostles group: thinkers such as Wedd, Dickinson, and McTaggart, and philosophers who later became famous such as Alfred North Whitehead, Bertrand Russell, and G. E. Moore. Among these names, G. E. Moore was all-important for these Cambridge intellectuals. From him Forster derived, as did his fellow Apostles, a conviction of the solid existence of the world perceived by the senses; an attitude of skepticism toward moral traditions; a compulsion to test such principles in actual circumstances, by the use of clarity and common sense; a passion for truth; and a high valuation of certain states of mind, those subsumed especially in personal relationships and in aesthetic satisfactions. Though Forster never read Moore at first hand, Moore's influence was strong upon him if indirect.

The Cambridge milieu helped form the Bloomsbury ethos, and the values that it represented were ones that were also crucial for Forster. Cambridge traditions encouraged the individual to express himself, but to express himself worthily. Flexibility, tolerance, and a disinterested inquiry into ethical and philosophical issues were all aspects of the humanism that Forster cherished, as they were of the philosophy that his fellows in the Bloomsbury Group advocated. Most of what Bloomsbury came to represent, Forster also valued: friendship, love of discussion, irreverence toward tradition and convention, agnosticism, the inevitability of social change, an appreciation of the new and the innovative in the arts, and a questioning of ready-made concepts to accord with the searching premises of a Moorean "realism." In some ways, possibly, Bloomsbury was not always serious enough for Forster, and he placed more emphasis upon the visionary and the transcendent than did most of those in the circle, with the possible exception of Virginia Woolf.

As to Forster's Bloomsbury affiliation, it is a subject of

minor controversy. All of his intimates in the circle stressed
that Forster was on its fringes rather than at its center. But they
always mentioned him. Those who regard Bloomsbury as
primarily the social phenomenon that it in large part was, tend
to deny Forster a place in the group since he did not live
permanently in London and so was at a remove from his
friends. But he knew the leading members of that set well, he
was friendly especially with Lytton Strachey and Leonard
Woolf, and he became a kind of mentor to Virginia Woolf. In
some senses he may have been a pioneer figure or a father figure
in Bloomsbury since he was slightly older than most in the
circle and had achieved a reputation before most of his com-
panions did. He had all but finished his career as novelist by the
time Virginia Woolf began hers; and Lytton Strachey did not
achieve notable success until *Eminent Victorians* (1918). Aside
from his friendships and the Cambridge milieu, Forster is to be
considered a Bloomsbury figure by virtue of his assimilation,
though at a remove, of G. E. Moore's ideas, some of which he
presented or dramatized in *The Longest Journey* and *Howards
End* and in the miscellaneous prose pieces written both before
and after the Great War. It would be difficult to think of
Bloomsbury without Forster (as Leon Edel does in a recent
book). [8] In addition to the links with Bloomsbury already
mentioned, there was the liberal and progressive temper revealed in *A Passage to India* and the centrality for Bloomsbury
of the concepts developed in the well-known "What I Believe." And possibly Forster's homosexual preferences
domesticated him in a circle in which variant forms of sexuality
were recognized as expressions of individuality.

Nathaniel Wedd suggested to Forster that he might write.
He acted on Wedd's suggestion and began by contributing
familiar and literary essays to the Cambridge undergraduate
magazine, *Basileona*. Thereafter, he contributed to the *Independent Review*, founded by Dickinson, Wedd, G. M. Trevelyan, and others, in protest against the imperialist policies of
Joseph Chamberlain. With Forster, the *Review* was important
as an organ for the expression of liberal ideas, as being "not so
much a Liberal review as an appeal to Liberalism from the Left

to be its better self." [9] Forster's contributions were not political, however, but were informal and biographical essays and some of his best stories, such as "The Road from Colonus" and "The Story of a Panic." In 1900 he received a Second Class in the Classical Tripos, Part I, under Nathaniel Wedd and in the next year a Second Class in the Historical Tripos, Part I, under Oscar Browning. On graduation from Cambridge, he began in October 1901 a year's travel to Italy, Sicily, and Austria in the company of his mother; and in the next year, 1903, he travelled alone on a cruise to Greece. At the suggestion of G. M. Trevelyan, he began in 1902 a connection as instructor at the Working Men's College in London, an affiliation that lasted off and on for twenty years.

The years from 1902 to 1910 might be regarded as the Jane Austen and George Meredith years in Forster's development, years in which he wrote, quite spontaneously, four novels, all of them revealing elements of greatness. During this time he was as deeply committed in his fiction to the society represented by his mother and her relatives as he was ironic and satiric at its expense. He thus revealed a tension and ambivalence toward it—dictated by affection and by clarity—that also characterized Jane Austen. From his general milieu and from foreign travel he derived the materials that he was to exploit in *A Room with a View* (1908; work on this novel in 1903 began his serious career) and *Where Angels Fear to Tread* (1905). Forster was both intensely immersed in upper-middle-class life in the Edwardian age and, in moments of honesty, intensely critical of it. The privileges of this society he enjoyed, but its repressive nature and its materialistic values he detested. At its best this regime could produce the lovable Honeychurches and the conscientious Emersons of *A Room with a View*; at its worst it could engender Mrs. Herriton and Harriet of *Where Angels Fear to Tread*, and Mrs. Failing, Mr. Elliot, and the Pembrokes of *The Longest Journey* (1907), all of whom reject "the holiness of the heart's imagination." [10] This aesthetic poise toward an order that sustained him at the same time that it exploited privilege, hypocrisy, and emotional evasion characterizes his work through *Howards End* (1910). The fact that

Forster was dominated by his mother and his aunts were undoubtedly repressive, but if it had not been for them Forster might not have found his subject so early.

What is really remarkable about the books is the passion in them, resulting perhaps from the lack of passion or the repression of it in Forster's life at the time. And this brings us to the second aspect of these books, their intense personal quality, their poetic fervor, their mythic overtones, and, on occasion, their visionary quality. This was the heritage from George Meredith and from Hardy, though Meredith, like Forster, combined the visionary with comedy. Forster's work, however, held more directness and less equivocation than Meredith's, and so Forster's blend of the transcendent and social comedy emerges fully as his own.

In any case, the right person had appeared at the right time to preserve this world in fiction, a writer with the capacity to enjoy a social order that he could also satirize and yet to perceive that a trivial and materialistic society might offer the resources for dramas of salvation. Forster's society was stable enough to survive his own criticisms of it, but it was not strong enough to survive the Great War, in the form that Forster had known it as a young man. In any event, the years from 1905 to 1910 were wonderful years of creative release and achievement for Forster, years in which his very inability perhaps to express himself emotionally to the fullest and to achieve sexual fulfillment provided him with a means whereby he could distance himself from his materials and attain an objective expression of his powers as writer and analyst of human behavior. Forster, the ironist, was in control of his inspiration, for the most part notably and successfully. When he expressed himself directly and wrote, as it were, from the heart, especially in *Maurice* (finished 1914; published 1971) and some of the homosexually oriented stories (published 1972), he was less steady and rigorous as artist. The conception of India as metaphor for the human condition gave him also that objectivity toward the experiences dramatized in *A Passage to India* (1924) that renders that book so memorable.

With *Howards End* Forster had arrived as a major writer, since the book received an almost universal acclaim. But he had difficulty writing fiction thereafter, as the solidity of the society that he had known so intimately dissipated, as his life with his mother became increasingly frustrating, as his homosexual temperament became more insistent, and as he tired of writing heterosexually-based marriage fiction. He began another novel, *Arctic Summer*, which was to explore the differences between the intellectual or civilized temperament and the heroic or chivalric. But after several attempts to get on with it, he abandoned it, partly because of his uncertainty as to how to actualize his heroic individual in a social setting, partly because of his inability to formulate the "major event" toward which the novel would move, partly because of the impossibility of dealing honestly with the homosexual implications in the situation, and partly because of other significant occurrences for him at the time.[11]

"A Struggle for Truer Values": Forster's Middle and Late Career

At least three events were of signal importance to Forster during the writing of *Howards End* and in the years immediately following.

First, occurred the meeting with Syed Ross Masood who became Forster's closest friend, an Indian for whom Forster acted as Latin tutor. The friendship was more intense on Forster's part, Masood being unable to respond to Forster's declarations of love. All the same, Masood opened up new experiences that were to take Forster beyond the Edwardian drawing room at home and life in a tourist's pension abroad. Largely as a result of Masood's influence, Forster was eager to see India which he visited for the first time in 1912–1913 in the company of G. L. Dickinson and R. C. Trevelyan.

The trip to India was the second important event in the years immediately preceding the Great War. Without the release and the enlargement that India provided, Forster could hardly have broken free of the parochialism of his culture and his own narcissistic tendencies. His six-month sojourn in India was truly a formative and liberating time for him. He was able to make firm a relationship with Sir Malcolm Darling, a British civil servant whom he had known earlier at King's College; and he visited Masood at Bankipore (the Chandrapore of *Passage*), enjoying the renewal of personal ties with him. He came to know well the Anglo-Indian servants of empire and the India that they controlled; and he also experienced princely India at first hand through his visits to the states of Chhatarpur and Dewas State Senior and through his friendships with the maharajahs of both principalities. India fired his imagination and he started working on *Passage* in 1913, writing most of "The Mosque" section and working his way toward the events in the "Caves" section; but he gave over the novel when war supervened. Forster also wrote a number of essays on Indian subjects for the *New Weekly*, which deserve to be better known.

The third event during these years was a visit in 1913 to Millthorpe to see Edward Carpenter, an advocate of an idealized homosexuality. When George Merrill, his companion, touched Forster on his posterior, Forster recognized, once for all, his own homosexual disposition.[12] The result was also an incursion of creative power, and Forster began his novel, *Maurice*, which he finished in a first draft in 1914. It was published in 1971 after his death.

World War I had momentous consequences for E. M. Forster, since it allowed him to reach sexual fulfillment for the first time, at Alexandria where he worked three years with the Red Cross as a "searcher" for missing soldiers. The relaxed atmosphere of the city encouraged him to seek a more active fulfillment than he had yet known. The result was his first satisfying sexual relationship, with an Egyptian tram conductor, Mohammed el Adl. Forster's compulsion was to seek gratification in a class other than his own, and this preference had perhaps prevented a full encounter previously with an individual from his own circle, with a man, for example, to whom he was once devoted, H. O. Meredith. The friendship with Mohammed was not only physical but affectionate in nature, a love affair as well as a sexual relationship. When war ended, Forster returned to England, after the marriage of Mohammed. On his way home in 1922 from a second trip to India Forster stopped to visit the now ailing Mohammed, who, in spite of the efforts to save him, died from consumption soon after Forster's departure. In Alexandria Forster also knew well the Greek poet, C. P. Cavafy, who established for him the provenance of the past over the present and whose reputation Forster, for the rest of his life, endeavored to promote in England. The literary results of these years were *Alexandria: A History and a Guide* and *Pharos and Pharillon*, the latter consisting of miscellaneous essays collected mostly from the *Egyptian Mail*. Forster gained in Egypt, moreover, some insights as to the conditions governing friendships between men of different races and classes, and he again observed the arrogance and intolerance of British servants of empire.

Forster's second trip to India took place in 1921. He went out as private secretary to the Maharajah of Dewas State Senior. The rewards and the frustrations involved in his employment were about equally divided, as we discern from Forster's account of his adventures in Dewas in *The Hill of Devi*. On this trip he again saw Masood, Sir Malcolm Darling, and the Majarajah of Chhatarpur and others of his earlier Indian acquaintances, though he was primarily based in Dewas. Here he witnessed the festivities associated with the birth of the god, Shri Krishna. This festival provided, in large part, the materials and the motifs for the concluding chapters of *A Passage to India*. He observed for himself, too, the disaffection that British administrators were producing among thoughtful Indians. It is possible, therefore, that without this second trip to India the writing of *Passage* might have come to a standstill. Leonard Woolf's encouragement was helpful to Forster in finishing his masterpiece, as were some letters sent him from Chhatarpur in 1923–1924 by J. R. Ackerley. The sympathy of T. E. Lawrence, whom Forster met in a significant way in 1924, was also important to him in the final states of composing his novel. Reviewers almost unanimously praised *A Passage to India* with the result that Forster's fame as a novelist was now incontestable.

More was expected from someone who had five impressive novels to his credit. Forster was aware of these expectations, but he also had doubts that he would be able to fulfill them. The disappearance of the cohesive society and the leisured

culture that he had known in Edwardian times and his reluc-
tance—or inability—to write about other than homosexual
themes caused him to disappoint those who were awaiting
other great things from him. He was able, however, to consoli-
date his reputation in another, but minor, way by delivering
the Clark Lectures at Trinity College, Cambridge, in 1927 and
publishing them in a book that has become a minor classic of
criticism, *Aspects of the Novel*. In 1924 Forster moved to West
Hackhurst, Abinger Hammer, when his mother inherited the
use of this property, where he lived until her death in 1945. The
house is the only known example of a building designed by
Forster's father, who planned it for his sister, Laura Forster.

Perhaps Forster's most notable development as writer during the last part of his career after *A Passage to India* was as an
essayist, as commentator on social problems, on political
issues, on books and the arts, on the past, on places including
the Orient, and on the menace of war. Always the point of
view was that of the engaged humanist, whereas the stance
varied from objective analysis of a situation, problem, or book
to exhortations for engaging in a specific action. The depth and
the sincerity of the utterances in *Abinger Harvest* and *Two
Cheers for Democracy* are only to be matched by their personal
quality. As an essayist on general subjects, Forster is, among
modern writers, second only to George Orwell, and he gener-
ates the same interest among his readers, though lacking
Orwell's range and decisiveness. Like Orwell, Forster defended liberal political and social values at a time when their
very existence was endangered, and, like Orwell, he was also
an engaging and perceptive literary critic.

As essayist, Forster became a public figure who stood increasingly as a spokesman for the committed intellectuals of
this period. In 1934–35 he was the president of the National
Council for Civil Liberties (he served again in 1942), and he
was especially instrumental in protesting the arbitrariness of
the Sedition Bill, which the Council, under Forster, succeeded
in discrediting. He participated in the International Congress
of Writers held in Paris in 1935 and delivered a speech, "Liberty in England" (*Abinger Harvest*), which represented his liberal credo but which the radicals of the Congress thought tepid.

He was tireless in protesting the Nazi menace abroad as that threatened to undermine the sanctity of the individual, his freedom and dignity. He was active also, at the beginning of World War II, in protecting speakers on the B.B.C. from censorship by the government or its representatives.

In his public utterances Forster remained loyal to standards that were his own—intellectual, aesthetic, personal, and ethical. When, during the Spanish Civil War, Julian Bell challenged him as to the adequacy of his philosophy, Forster replied that he was unable to change the habits of sixty years and that he would continue to be "gentle, semi-idealistic and semi-cynical, kind, tolerant, demure" [13]—in short, a liberal and a humanist. His humanism, however, was more than a habit of mind, and Bell perhaps did not fully realize this fact. It became a strengthening personal and ethical philosophy during a time of international upheaval, a philosophy that at once sustained himself and provided an inspiriting example for others, as Christopher Isherwood testified in *Down There on a Visit*: ". . . he's far saner than anyone else I know. And immensely, superhumanly strong. He's strong because he doesn't try to be a stiff-lipped stoic, like the rest of us, and so he'll never crack. He's absolutely flexible. He lives by love, not by will. . . . He and his books and what they stand for are all that is truly worth saving from Hitler; and the vast majority of people on this island aren't even aware that he exists." [14]

The relationship with Isherwood, an active homosexual, though he was never involved with Forster in an affair, suggests the other aspect of Forster's life beginning with the 1920s, an aspect that was not known in any complete way until the publication of P. N. Furbank's *E. M. Forster: A Life* (1977, 1978). In the late 1920s, as a result of the efforts of solicitous friends like J. R. Ackerley and Sebastian Sprott, Forster's personal life began to enlarge. Through Ackerley he met, first, Harry Daley and became his lover for a few years; and then Bob Buckingham, a policeman and thereafter a probation officer, a man of some literary and cultural interests. In any event, Bob became Forster's closest friend after the 1930 meeting. How active this relationship was remains a question, since Furbank reports that Bob was shocked when Forster, near

death, admitted that he was homosexual and had had a sexual
as well as a friendly interest in Bob. Bob's disclaimer is not easy
to credit entirely, but on Forster's side homoerotic feeling
certainly prevailed. Bob's marriage to May Hockey in 1932
tested the relationship between himself and Forster. After
considerable strain, May and Forster lived to accept each other
and to become fast friends; in fact, Forster would not relinquish her hand when, on his death bed, he was still conscious.
There were other more casual encounters arranged for him by
Daley and others in his circle, though the promiscuity of men
like Ackerley alienated Forster, who desired relationships of
some durability. He was saddened in 1937 by the death of his
two closest Indian friends, Syed Ross Masood and the Maharajah of Dewas State Senior.

It is important to keep in perspective Forster's contacts with
men from the lower class, some of whom were disreputable,
because, in counterpoint with his sexual compulsions, went
Forster's active, continuing intellectual existence and his full
commitment to humanistic values and to the life of the mind
and spirit in times of economic and political crisis.

Because Forster had become inadvertently involved in a libel
suit as the result of an essay in the first printing of *Abinger
Harvest*, he was inhibited from publishing a book for fifteen
years, if we can except incidental lectures and minor efforts
such as his pageants. The war also acted as an inhibiting influence upon Forster, the writer. He lived with his ailing mother
throughout the war at West Hackhurst, a property that Lily
Forster enjoyed the use of during her life but which was to
revert to its owner, Lord Farrer, on her death. Any chance that
Forster might have had to stay there after Lily's death in 1945,
he removed by his own ineptitude when it came to negotiations
with the Farrer family. And yet, by and large, our sympathies
lie with Forster in his continuing imbroglio with the Farrers, a
situation supplying some of the most amusing pages in Furbank's biography of Forster.[15]

On the whole, the removal from West Hackhurst was more
liberating than might have been thought at the time. When
Cambridge University offered him a resident fellowship, Forster's problem was solved. The move to Cambridge was fortu-

nate because he was no longer so isolated as he would have been had he continued at West Hackhurst. Instead, he became one of the centers of life at King's College and perhaps the most celebrated figure at the University. Then followed an upsurge in his reputation with the publication of Lionel Trilling's *E. M. Forster* in 1943 (London, 1944). Trilling's book coincided with a time spirit that was responsive to Forster's novels and to his general outlook:

Forster's humanism and liberalism spoke directly to those who were fighting to preserve the traditions of Western civilization. His offhand, ironic, understated manner appealed to a generation of intellectuals alienated by the pretentious and by the irrational appeals to the mass psyche prevalent in the 1930s and the 1940s. His sardonic, somber, intermittently cynical, and sometimes tragic world view (with its recognition of the evil forces in man's nature and the disparity between his aspirations and his limited capabilities) and, above all, his projection of an imaginative world in his fiction notable for its aesthetic beauty, consistency, and lucidity appealed to a world beleaguered by war and the problems engendered by its aftermath.[16]

He became the object of much homage, but he was also cordial to the Cambridge undergraduates and to visitors from outside.

It was a time, moreover, of creativity. He was able to complete one of his best stories, "The Other Boat"; he gave a final revision to *Maurice*; he collaborated with Eric Crozier in writing the libretto for Benjamin Britten's masterly opera, *Billy Budd*, based on Herman Melville's novel; he wrote many essays which deserve to be collected, some on a par with the best in *Abinger Harvest* and *Two Cheers for Democracy*; and he composed two books of much interest and charm if of less weight than his fiction, *The Hill of Devi* (1953) and *Marianne Thornton: A Domestic Biography* (1956). In the first, Forster principally gathered his letters written home from India, and gave some running commentary on them. As a result, *Devi* is a source book for, and gloss upon, his greatest novel. In the second book, Forster paid homage to the Thornton relative who had done the most for him, and he provides us, incidentally, with some vivid re-creations of life in the nineteenth-century British upper middle class.

Forster continued to make himself felt as a public presence, testifying in behalf of D. H. Lawrence's *Lady Chatterley's Lover* at the time of the censorship trial involving that book in 1960; acting as president of the Cambridge University Humanist Federation; reviewing regularly, for Ackerley's *Listener*, books on India and many other subjects; writing letters to the press on such subjects as *apartheid*, capital punishment, and the Chinese invasion of India;[17] and expressing much concern for the dangers that Europe would continue to face from a potential atomic holocaust. He was able to cultivate new friends and old ones and, until far along in his residence at Cambridge, to do much travelling, notably two trips to America (in 1947 and 1949), about which he was enthusiastic. There had also been an excursion to India in 1945, Forster's third, to attend the P. E. N. Conference at Jaipur. For him the enchantment and mystery of India had faded somewhat in face of the obsession with politics that he then noted.[18]

In his later years Forster increasingly became a man of letters and a public figure of importance who carried on aggressively his protest against the repressions of the modern age at home and against political totalitarianism abroad. When a new war threatened, Forster had begun to feel in 1938 that all was lost except "personal affection, the variety of human conduct, the importance of truth."[19] This humanistic ideal was not lost but it was in peril. In his columns in *Time and Tide* ("Notes on the Way") written in 1934 and 1935, he spoke out against the political and social ills and oppressions of the time. Forster delineated his own contribution when, in writing for this journal, he speculated about the role of the intellectual in forming a climate of opinion for current issues, such as war, rearmament, fascism, and communism. Forster's matured opinion was that it did "matter just a little," if the intellectual were socially conscientious.

Forster himself ended by being a sage and a powerful figure for his contemporaries, precisely because he felt that what he had to say mattered "a little," even if it did not matter too much.[20] He expressed his hopes and fears for what they were and had the grace to eschew propaganda. His tenacity, his intellectual flexibility, his sense of incongruity, his modesty, and his integrity made of him a symbolic figure for the intellectuals of the 1930s and the World War II era, as they tried to determine the aspects of liberal culture that they would try to champion in confronting the Nazi menace; and these same qualities accounted, too, for his postwar reputation. In such a connection we can also refer to his 1940 utterance as to the purpose of mankind: it is engaged, he said, in an inner or religious struggle as well as an outer or political one, in "a struggle for truer values, a struggle of the individual towards the dark, secret place where he may find reality." [21] Forster meant so much to his contemporaries by virtue of the intensity with which he himself pursued such a quest.

We now turn to a consideration, principally, of Forster the writer of fiction. This is a rewarding enterprise, since his novels and short stories are the works in which his creative powers attained their greatest strength. While focusing primarily upon his fiction, we can recognize that he was a man of letters whose achievement is varied and whose work is greater in bulk and quality than critics have sometimes thought. Yet it is the fascination exerted by his novels that makes the devotee return to Forster so constantly, so conscientiously, and so enthusiastically.

Chapter Two

The Italian Novels and the Early Short Stories

"A Sense of Deities Reconciled": *A Room with a View*

Forster began *A Room with a View* (1908) before *Where Angels Fear to Tread* (1905) and finished it after *The Longest Journey* (1907).[1] Since it is the most halcyon and direct of his novels and since it was the work with which he started, we shall begin with it. Though it is his least complex book, it is his most Jane Austen-like and perhaps his most delightful. As in the earlier-published *Angels*, Italy acts as the chief source of vitality, and the two novels reflect the intense impact that the South made upon him in his early twenties. In *Room*, after the characters return to England in Part II, Italy retreats to the background but still acts as a formative influence.

In any case, Italy is the main force which in Part I of *Room* contributes to Lucy Honeychurch's liberation. The conventional Reverend Beebe reluctantly acknowledges the intuitive wisdom of Italians though it chiefly annoys him: "They pry everywhere, they see everything, and they know what we want before we know it ourselves."[2] So "Phaethon," the driver of the carriage taking the English to the hills above Florence, reads Lucy's heart and directs her to George Emerson rather than to the Reverends Beebe and Eager when she asks in faltering Italian "where the good men are." Both Italy and the English countryside encourage a free and open existence as compared to cramped, stereotyped, middle-class British life. The primary impression produced by the novel, the prevalence of wind and air and sunlight, establishes, as in George Meredith, the primary role of nature as redemptive power.

The English and Italian settings, rendered with complete

18

immediacy, reveal Forster's sensitivity to place. Houses and buildings take on life in his fiction: the church of Santa Croce and the Pension Bertolini in Florence, for example, and Windy Corner, a Surrey country house. The Florentine pension and the Surrey house focus the action in the two sections of the novel. Chapter 1 presents at the Pension almost all the actors who figure in Part I: Lucy; Charlotte Bartlett, her "proper" chaperone; George Emerson, a troubled but vital young man; his father, the prophetic proponent of the free and natural life like that advocated by the American Ralph Waldo Emerson; the Reverend Mr. Beebe, the ascetically inclined but socially agreeable clergyman of Summer Street near Windy Corner; Eleanor Lavish, an "emancipated" novelist whose unconventionality is superficial; and the Misses Alan, elderly and genteel lady travellers. Only the snobbish chaplain to the English colony, the Reverend Cuthbert Eager, remains for Chapter 5.

The opening chapter of Part II introduces at Windy Corner all the other principals: Mrs. Honeychurch, Lucy's impulsive and affectionate mother and an endearing portrait of Forster's maternal grandmother whom he loved intensely; Freddy, Lucy's playful but instinctively sound brother; and Cecil Vyse, a "medieval" young man to whom Lucy has become engaged after his third proposal. She breaks her engagement when Mr. Emerson convinces her that she really loves his son. In the concluding chapter, Lucy and George return for their honeymoon to the Pension Bertolini which provides a frame for the novel and a reminder of Italy's pervasive power.

Structure depends upon a number of encounters between Lucy and George which revise her staid outlook. In Chapter I the Emersons offer the ladies their room with a view; and, before retiring, the now restless Lucy gazes beyond the Arno at the hills which betoken the freedom that she has not yet achieved. In Chapter 2 George appears in the Church of Santa Croce at his most lugubrious, and Lucy disdainfully pities him; but in Chapter 4 he reveals his potential strength as he supports her in his arms when she faints after witnessing a quarrel between two Italians over money, a quarrel that results in the sudden murder of one of them. After Lucy's "rescue," she and George gaze at the Arno flowing beneath them and respond to its mystery and promise (though with her rational mind, Lucy is later ashamed that she has given herself away to this extent). With the death of the Italian, Lucy feels that she, too, has "crossed some spiritual boundary," though she is not sure at the moment just what it may be. When they go back to Florence for their honeymoon, it is as if to place themselves under the spell of a force—the river—that has never ceased to exert itself. In Italy violence enlarges Lucy's horizons, and she now feels that something has indeed "happened to the living."

In Chapter 4 Forster also suggests the effete quality of the casual tourist's culture when Lucy buys photographs of works by the great masters. Reality impinges upon the pictures when the dying man's blood spatters them and when George throws them into the Arno to have them, as it were, washed pure in its waters. The principal picture, Botticelli's *The Birth of Venus*, has symbolic meaning that is at once lucid and profound. The picture connects with the Italian springtime, the pagan atmosphere of the novel, and the birth of love in Lucy's soul. Just as the blood of the murdered man defiles the pictures, so Lucy would, through her own blindness and obstinacy, do violence to her instincts. Just as the soiled photographs return to the water that has given birth to Venus, so Lucy must immerse herself in elemental passion, in order to cleanse her soul and to attain a new life. The birth of the goddess and the death of the Italian man also suggest the nearness of love and death as the most fundamental and mysterious of our experiences.

Lucy has another encounter with George when in Chapter 6 the Bertolini guests go for a drive above Fiesole. Lucy discovers that her standards have altered and that she does not know how to account for the change. She doubts that Miss Lavish is an artist and that Mr. Beebe is spiritual, but previously she would have been less critical. She judges them by a new criterion. Vital energy, she thinks, should animate them, but she finds them lacking in warmth and spontaneity, qualities that she has begun unconsciously to associate with George. Lucy is a woman who registers the effects of an emotional awakening before she can acknowledge its existence and cause. The Arno Valley is once more present in the distance from above Fiesole when George kisses Lucy after she surprises him on the bank covered with violets. Going against the dictates of instinct, Lucy seeks the advice of her proper chaperone, Miss Bartlett, who dismisses George, and the ladies depart forthwith from Rome where Lucy first meets Cecil Vyse.

Encounters with George also organize the narrative in Part II, although in the first chapters it is Cecil Vyse, Lucy's fiancé (or "fiasco" as Freddy calls him), who dominates. Another kiss, Cecil's self-conscious one in Chapter 9, contrasts with George's spontaneous embraces. Cecil not only takes the place temporarily of George as his temperamental opposite, but assumes in Part II the role of Charlotte Bartlett as exemplar of the proprieties. In Chapter 12 Lucy regains contact with George as he emerges like a pagan god from "The Sacred Lake," a charming country pool near Windy Corner, and emanates all of nature's freshness.

Part II is a contest between George and Cecil for the control of Lucy's inner being. In Chapter 15 a kiss again enlivens the novel. George has just beaten Lucy at tennis; while the contestants rest, Cecil reads from Miss Lavish's novel, which features an incident similar to George's first kissing of Lucy on the heights over Florence. Miss Lavish had learned of the incident through the duplicity of Charlotte Bartlett who had enjoined Lucy to tell no one about it, even her mother. The memory of this scene arouses George, and he kisses Lucy in a copse close to Windy Corner. The outraged Lucy again does violence to her true self; she retreats from the light of truth and passion and prepares to enter "the vast armies of the benighted" (p. 204). After this second kiss and the lies that she tells about herself to George, Cecil, Mr. Beebe, her mother, and Mr. Emerson, pretense all but conquers her. In Florence, after George's kiss, she had realized how difficult it was to be truthful, but by this point she has become less conscientious.

The overall movement of the novel results in enlightenment for Lucy, after several divagations into falsehood. With one side of her nature she responds to passion as it concenters in George; with another, she aligns herself with upholders of Victorian social standards, Charlotte Bartlett and Cecil Vyse. With unremitting force Lucy's instincts carry her toward a larger life than these mentors will allow. Finally, Mr. Emerson sweeps away her accumulated errors of perception when he divines her love for George, instructs her about the sanctity of passion, and gives her the courage to claim the man she loves.

From the beginning Italy is a subversive influence, causing Lucy's well-known world to break up; and in its place the "magic city" of Florence elicits all that is unpredictable. Passionate, vibrant, violent Italy all but overwhelms Lucy. Her sympathies for "Phaethon," the coach-driver, startle her, as he embraces his "Persephone" on the drive to Fiesole. If she had been able to see more clearly, she would have recognized a god in George Emerson, who would, for his part, have seen in a liberated Lucy a real goddess. Before he kissed her in the hills, she had seemed "as one who had fallen out of heaven" (80); and, before her inhibitions stifled her, Lucy could identify him with "heroes—gods—the nonsense of schoolgirls" (85). Later when she greets him at "The Sacred Lake," she thinks of herself as bowing "to gods, to heroes, to the nonsense of school girls! She had bowed across the rubbish that cumbers the world" (155). And George was here a "Michelangelesque" figure, the essence of heroic vitality; earlier he had similarly appeared to her as a figure appropriate to "the ceiling of the Sistine Chapel, carrying a burden of acorns" (29). But, in repudiating George a second time, she turns from a god incarnate to the academic study of Greek mythology as she prepares for her journey to Greece with the Misses Alan. She is rejecting in the actuality a god, knowledge of whose counterparts she is pursuing in the abstract.[3]

In order to intensify Lucy's conflict with convention and to convey the force of her muted passion, Forster uses imagery drawn from music.[4] Music lifts her out of herself and permits her to see, at least for the moment, the irrelevance of prescriptive standards: "She was then no longer either deferential or patronizing; no longer either a rebel or a slave" (34). By force of will, she transforms Beethoven's tragic sonatas, for example, into expressions of triumph. Lucy, moreover, instinctively suits her music to her mood or situation. In Italy where she can acknowledge the elemental, she leans toward Beethoven. When she plays for Cecil and his guests in London, she performs the decorous Schumann, who suggests to her "the sadness of the incomplete." It is as if she has some intimations that she is now denying the demands of life, and so cannot play her beloved Beethoven in these artificial surroundings. At Windy Corner she plays the erotic garden music from Gluck's *Armide* and makes her audience restless (as if they reflect her own conflicts), and she also finds it impossible to play the sensual garden sequence from *Parsifal* in George's presence, since she is sexually distraught at this time. When she plans to renounce the call of passion, she indulges in the artifices (for her) of Mozart.

Forster suggests Lucy's progress toward enlightenment in terms of light and shadow images (these are so numerous that full discussion is not possible). Light and darkness suffuse natural phenomena, as these respectively signify freedom and inner fulfillment or bondage and human waywardness. Forster also associates light with the Emersons to the extent that father and son represent spiritual truth. In Italy Mr. Emerson urges Lucy to expose her thoughts to the sunlight rather than keep them in the depths of her nature. She resists full illumination, however, because she resists as yet the full promptings of instinct. George is, like Lucy, in danger of spiritual disablement, and he will enter the abyss if Lucy does not return his love, his father tells her in England. Lucy, in fact, will condemn herself by her evasions and lies to "marching in the armies of darkness" (212), so long as she resists the truth about herself.

Though the clouds of pessimism often surround George, he becomes a source of light to Lucy. Both darkness and bright light characterize her encounter with him in the Piazza Signoria. To correspond with the crime that takes place there, the Piazza is in shadow and the tower of the palace arises out of a sinister gloom. Yet the tower is emblematic of the sexuality that Lucy experiences and represses, rising as it does "out of the lower darkness like a pillar of roughened gold. It seemed no longer a tower, no longer supported by earth, but some unattainable treasure throbbing in the tranquil sky" (48). In Surrey George's kindness to his father strikes Lucy as "sunlight touching a vast landscape—a touch of the morning sun" (177). He has just said that "there is a certain amount of

falsehd — victorian society (bourgeois)
truth — living an honest life
not independence but interdependence.

24   E. M. FORSTER

kindness, just as there is a certain amount of light," and that one "should stand in it for all you are worth, facing the sunshine." When he wins at tennis from Lucy, he is brilliant against the sunlight, godlike in appearance. In defending himself in Surrey after he kisses her, he emphasizes how his love had been kindled when he saw her the day that he bathed in the Sacred Lake; the life-giving water and the glorious sunlight combined to make her beauty overwhelming. It is with this sunlight, too, that Forster identifies George and suggests that he is a Phaethon figure.

After she breaks the engagement with Cecil, Lucy realizes that George has gone into darkness; but she does not yet perceive that by her denial of sex she is fashioning an "armour of falsehood" (189) and is about to go into darkness herself. She now becomes as one who sins "against passion and truth" (204), or against Eros and Pallas Athena. She resists taking others into her confidence lest inner exploration result in self-knowledge and "that king of terrors—Light" (225), the light that her own name (from the Latin, *lux*, meaning light) signifies and that she must acknowledge to become her true self. But for the intervention of Mr. Emerson, Lucy would stay in darkness. He gives her "a sense of deities reconciled" (240); he enables her, in short, to balance the claims of Eros and Pallas Athena, of sense and soul.

George, who is in part a nature god, is at his most vital seen against the expanses of the Florentine and English hills. Appropriately enough, his earliest memory is the inspiriting landscape seen from Hindhead in company with his mother and father, a prospect which unified the family in deepest understanding. In symbolic terms, both the Emersons now have, and have always had, "the view" that Lucy must acquire. External nature is always seen in motion, as if it too is in protest against Cecil's static existence and in sympathy with George's dynamic energies. Kinetic and auditory images dominate so that nature seems always active rather than passive. The Arno River after a storm bounds on like a lion, and at several points it murmurs a promise of a free and open existence for the lovers. In Surrey and Sussex the atmosphere, comprising "the intolerable tides of heaven," is always in motion. Glorious lateral views dominate the region; but this landscape becomes ominous as Lucy represses sexual passion. The sounds and movements of nature intensify to register their protest as Lucy denies life and love. Now the sky goes wild; the winds roar through pine trees; and gray clouds, charging across the heavens, obscure the white ones and the blue sky, "as the roaring tides of darkness" set in. The novel closes on a serene note, however, with nature's forces finding fruition in human beings, as Lucy on her honeymoon surrenders not only to George but to the Florentine spring and to the Arno's whispers.

When Mr. Emerson counsels Lucy toward the novel's end, he emphasizes the difficulties of life, the continual presence of muddles, and the consequent need to clear them away; he quotes a friend of his (actually Samuel Butler): [5] "Life is a public performance on the violin, in which you must learn the instrument as you go along" (236). Lucy acquires now a sense of the complexities of life; and she finds that she cannot plan for it and know in advance its contingencies. This lesson she learns from her first meeting with George in Surrey, for she had not thought of meeting him when he is happy and exuberant, as a godlike being at the Sacred Lake against the background of verdant nature. Lucy herself shines with intensity throughout the novel, with the result that a rather ordinary young woman is transfigured into a radiant presence, the resolution of whose conflicts becomes a matter of genuine urgency.

George is designedly less complex than Lucy, since he need not so much modify his values as gain the courage to assert them. Early in the novel George gives Lucy "the feeling of greyness, of tragedy that might only find solution in the night" (29), though Forster fails to establish the precise intellectual grounds for his pessimism. Forster misses in George some opportunity to convey the complicated mentality of a young man suffering from a *Weltschmerz* characteristic of the late Victorian age and induced, among other forces, by the loss of a dynamic religious faith. But George is, on the whole, a successful creation, an archetypal personage embodying the freshness, the power, and the passion of youth.

Lucy's chief mentor and George's father, Mr. Emerson, evinces a rousing candor that is refreshing, but on the whole Forster conceived him with less decisiveness and complexity than the novel demands. His valetudinarianism, for example, is too far removed from the vitality attributed to him, and his message is too direct to be aesthetically compelling. But what damages Mr. Emerson as a presence chiefly is the dated quality of some of his ideas, ideas which reveal how shallow he is when he assumes that he is being profound. In his scathing remarks about the Reverend Eager's Giotto lecture, in the Church of Santa Croce, Mr. Emerson exhibits a literalness of mind not far different from the fundamentalism he criticizes. Thus, he asserts that an edifice built by faith means that the workmen were underpaid and that Giotto's *Ascension of Saint John* is ridiculous because a "fat man in blue" could not be "shooting into the sky like an air-balloon" (27). It is therefore difficult to agree with Forster that Mr. Emerson is "profoundly religious," for he seems to operate on the surface, rather than at the depths, of religious issues.

Forster's great success in the novel is with his rendition of the humorous and satirically envisioned persons. Some of them—the Reverend Eager, Mrs. Honeychurch, and Eleanor Lavish—Forster presents in brief, through epigrammatic summary or through their spoken words. He tells us, for instance, all we have to know of Reverend Eager, in this account of his unctuous ministrations for transient visitors: ". . . it was his avowed custom to select those of his migratory sheep who seemed worthy, and give them a few hours in the pastures of the permanent" (59). The portrait is made complete when Eager discourses patronizingly upon the way in which the "lower-class" Emersons have risen: "Generally, one has only sympathy with their success. The desire for education and for social advance—in these things there is something not wholly vile. There are some working men whom one would be very willing to see out here in Florence—little as they would make of it" (62). Reverend Eager's apparent generosity, in fact, masks feelings of snobbishness, contempt, and exclusiveness.

But it is with Lucy's antagonists that Forster does best: Charlotte Bartlett and Cecil Vyse. Although he presents them satirically, he also sees them sympathetically; as a result, his humor at their expense is genial as well as satiric. Charlotte and Cecil are misguided, they are hypocrites, and they extinguish the generous instincts; they cause unhappiness and they propagate darkness. But, since they are not conscious of wrongdoing, Forster not only tolerates them but feels affection for them. As a consequence, he fully delineates them; and they become large-scale figures even if they are not complex individuals who develop dynamically.

Charlotte is given to excessive propriety and is deficient, therefore, in graciousness, kindness, and consideration. Her hypocrisies are the source of much fine comedy, as is her penchant for the irrelevant. Specious and superficial incidents and ideas gain ascendancy in her mind and allow her thereby to evade uncomfortable realities that a conscientious individual would feel obliged to face.[6] She is able to rationalize any occurrence in her own favor. Thus she stresses Miss Lavish's perfidy in using for her novel Lucy's being kissed by George on the Florentine heights. As a result, Charlotte diverts attention from her own perfidy in telling Miss Lavish in the first place: "Never again shall Eleanor Lavish be friend of mine" (191). Her incompetence as a person who is "practical without ability" is the source of much humor. Her packing in Florence is protracted further than it ought to be, she is unable to pay the driver at Windy Corner because she arrives without small change and then becomes confused in her monetary calculations, and she "impedes" Mrs. Honeychurch with offers of help in tying up dahlias after a night of storm. Her sense of decorum is outlandish, as she recoils from George's casual mention in Chapter 1 that his father "is in his bath," and only she could be quite so thorough a martyr in her home to a "tiresome" boiler.

The portrait of Cecil is equally authoritative. He is the diffident man who finds it difficult to become emotionally involved even with an attractive woman. Forster describes him as resembling a "fastidious saint" in the façade of a French cathedral and as being by temperament self-conscious and ascetic. His courtship follows the arc from "patronizing civility" to "a profound uneasiness." The uneasiness arises

Cecil the egoist
= Britain the egoist
(as shown in other
Forster novels)

when Lucy threatens to become vital and dynamic, to be more
than a Leonardesque work of art. Cecil calls himself a disciple
of George Meredith, agreeing with his mentor that the cause of
comedy and the cause of truth are identical, though Cecil
cannot realize that he will be the individual, in the course of his
engagement to Lucy, to be unmasked as self-server and hypocrite.

George Emerson appraises well his adversary. He perceives
that Cecil "kills," when it comes to people, by misjudging or
undervaluing them, by playing tricks on them instead of cher-
ishing "the most sacred form of life that he can find" (194), and
by being snobbish and supercilious toward those inferior to
him in station and income. Accordingly, Cecil patronizes
Lucy when she confuses two Italian painters, winces when Mr.
Emerson mispronounces the names of artists, becomes bored
and disdainful of the Honeychurches for whom "eggs, boilers,
hydrangeas, maids" form part of reality, and fails to see that it
is sometimes an act of kindness for a bad player to make a
fourth at tennis. In short, as with Meredith's Sir Willoughby
Patterne, Cecil is an egoist, with the egoist's inability to see
himself as he is, with the egoist's tendency to assume that other
people exist to minister to his well-being. Something of the
large dimensions of Sir Willoughby inheres in Cecil's portrait,
though Lucy hardly attains the dimensions of Clara Middleton, her prototype in *The Egoist*.

Northrop Frye's discussion of the *mythos* of comedy illuminates *A Room with a View* which is the only Forster narrative that can be fully assimilated to these ideas of Frye's.[7] This
mythos devolves about the central characters' attainment of a
new society after the influence of those who obstruct their free
development has been neutralized (Charlotte Bartlett and
Cecil Vyse are the "blocking" figures in *Room*). There trans-
pires a new life for the hero and the heroine as they move
"from a society controlled by habit, ritual bondage, arbitrary
law and the older characters to a society controlled by youth
and pragmatic freedom," under the aegis of "a benevolent
grandfather,"—Mr. Emerson in this novel. There also occurs a
visit to "the green world" of romance, to the healing powers of
nature, as George and Lucy participate in their ritualistic hon-

eymoon beside the life-restoring Arno River before they return, reinvigorated, to middle-class life in England. If anything, the mythic and archetypal—and romance—aspects of
Forster's imagined universe are even more to the fore in his
subsequent fiction.

"Midway in Our Life's Journey": *Where Angels Fear to Tread*

Forster's novels, as we have intimated, reveal an expert
fusing of the real and the archetype, which one of his critics has
defined as "a mythic symbol." [8] On the one side, as a writer of
social comedy and realism, Forster descends from Jane Austen. On the other side, he is a writer of romance, wherein
characters and situations assume extended proportions that
carry them beyond observable reality to the general, the archetypal, and the mythic; and here Forster descends from the
Brontës and Thomas Hardy and evinces similarities to D. H.
Lawrence. Forster also has affinities with George Meredith,
and his fiction, like Meredith's, includes these contrasting
strands. In the romance, characters are not only realistically
envisioned but symbolical, even allegorical constructs; and
they pursue such elemental activities as the quest for truth, the
search for mystical transcendence, the aspiring toward visionary experience, the effort to achieve rapport with nature, and
the struggle with good or evil. In this last respect, Forster's
characters tend to be dynamic embodiments of good, of evil,
or a mixture of the two. In Forster's fusion of realism and
romance he attains his true distinction and originality. His
novels are like Jane Austen's except for what they share with
Hardy's and Lawrence's; and they are like Hardy's and Lawrence's except for what they share with Jane Austen's.

The formulations of Northrop Frye also help define the
scope and nature of Forster's fiction. With respect to Frye's
discussions of the *mythoi* of comedy (spring), romance (summer), tragedy (autumn), and irony and satire (winter), Forster's fiction most nearly approximates the *mythos* of romance
(though it contains elements from the other *mythoi* as well). In
the romance the protagonist, according to Frye, engages in a

perilous journey, undergoes a crucial struggle with antagonistic forces, and achieves a certain exaltation as a result of the
survival of a test. In *Where Angels Fear to Tread* both Philip
Herriton and Caroline Abbott undertake not only a physical
journey but, without always realizing it, a spiritual journey to
regions previously unknown to them. In some instances the
protagonist achieves his triumph through one who dies that
others might live more fully; the baby's death in *Angels*
perhaps serves this function as does Rickie Elliott's death in
The Longest Journey. The quest often involves a victory of
fertility over the waste land (as in the concluding section of *A
Passage to India* where the monsoon rains work their soothing
spell, as a result in part of Mrs. Moore who is ritually sacrificed
to the ocean); and elements of increased awareness, rebirth,
and resurrection are associated with romance as Frye conceives
of it and as Forster exemplifies it in his fiction. In *Angels* Philip
and Caroline undertake such a quest and emerge with new
knowledge of themselves and their world, and are in fact
"reborn."

Some readers would agree with one recent critic that *Where
Angels Fear to Tread* and *A Passage to India* represent Forster's
artistry at its most controlled and inspired.[9] *Angels* is, in any
case, a remarkable first novel and, at the very least, a minor
classic of the Edwardian age. For a short book, its scope is
broad: it presents a contrast in national types, an analysis of
various temperaments from the middle class, a comedy of
manners exposing the hypocrisies of this class, a romance in
which forces of evil oppose those of good, and a tragedy
originating in the substitution of convention for charity and
imagination.

The novel divides into two main sections, each focusing on
an Italian journey which Philip Herriton undertakes, as
spokesman for his suburban Sawston family. On his first trip
he hopes to prevent his widowed sister-in-law, Lilia, from
marrying Gino Carella, a dentist's son in the mountain village
of Monteriano; but he arrives too late. Lilia's friend, Caroline
Abbott, had helped arrange the marriage; and she eventually
becomes the heroine as she moves from Sawston's bourgeois
values to a more open life in Italy. As for the shallow Lilia,

Gino humiliates her and is unfaithful; and somewhat later she escapes an intolerable life with him by dying in childbirth.

On his second journey to Italy at the behest of his mother Philip wishes to negotiate with Gino about adopting the latter's baby boy. Caroline Abbott has also gone again to Italy for the same purpose; she hopes to atone for her part in encouraging Lilia's disastrous marriage by devoting herself to the child. Both Philip and Caroline give over their plans to get control of the baby when they realize the depth of Gino's paternal passion. They fail to reckon with the evil genius of Philip's single-minded sister Harriet, however, who kidnaps the baby without Philip's sanction. The carriage in which the Herritons leave Monteriano for the station in the valley overturns during a rainstorm in a collision with a carriage taking Caroline away also; the baby is killed and Philip's arm broken. When he brings news of the disaster to Gino, Gino tortures him by alternately twisting his arm and suffocating him. Caroline comes upon them in time to save Philip, and she manages, with her goddess-like dignity, to reconcile the men by having them drink ritualistically of the milk that the servant had prepared for the now-dead baby. Although Caroline has by this time succumbed to Gino's sexual warmth, she is unable to reveal her love to him. Philip's own dawning love for her is deflected when on the train ride home from Italy she confesses to him her unrequited passion for Gino. If Philip and Caroline are both unfulfilled, they have become aware, through the liberating influence of Italy, of possibilities heretofore unknown to them.

The idea of the life-pilgrimage is central in the book. The opening lines from *The Divine Comedy*, which Gino quotes in the second chapter, inform us that in "the middle of life's journey" [10] the poet Dante felt most deeply the weight of his destiny but also experienced the revelation that brought him peace. The two central characters—Philip and Caroline—are likewise some distance along in their lives. They then undergo profound disturbances as the novel progresses; and they eventually return—but greatly altered—to the "true way" that they had either lost or never fully known.

Until his publishers intervened, Forster had intended to

name his book "Monteriano" as if to emphasize that he had found his structural principle in what Italy signifies to his characters. Italy is the background presence, and the characters achieve awareness and value to the degree that they can relate to it. On his second trip Philip arrives at the truth that Italy embodies. He and Caroline Abbott have been "converted" to the South, partly by appreciating the exuberance of the audience for a performance of *Lucia di Lammermoor*. At this point Philip is looking out at the Piazza and suddenly comprehends the unity that Monteriano, as a microcosm of all Italy, represents: "the Palazzo Pubblico, the Collegiate Church, and the Caffè Garibaldi: the intellect, the soul, and the body" (146).

Philip follows a vacillating course toward enlightenment, as the force exerted by Italy either fails to affect him or else stirs him deeply. On his earlier travels his confrontation with Italy had been aesthetic rather than moral; he had yet to learn "that human love and love of truth sometimes conquer where love of beauty fails" (69). He has been unable to remold or to reject Sawston; with the failure of this prophetic aestheticism, he indulges in sardonic humor toward Sawston and its people. His fascination with Italy and his negative appraisal of Sawston last until Lilia decides to marry Gino. His repudiation of Gino—and Italy—demonstrates that his understanding and his unconventionality had been superficial. Yet one can measure Philip's total progress in terms of his appreciation for the spontaneous and life-infusing Italian values and of his revulsion from the proprieties and hypocrisies of Sawston.

As soon as Philip reaches Italy on his second journey, the spell of the South begins to work. Although he regards the railroad station at Florence as the center of "beastly Italy," he even now feels that "enchantment" lurks beneath the surface of his discomfiting experiences. When he gets to Monteriano, he succumbs reluctantly to its charm while his sister Harriet decisively isolates herself from it. He is aware, however, that Italy can still expose him to ridicule when, for instance, he makes a child-guide unhappy by overpaying her. But when Caroline conveys to him Gino's regrets for his former rudeness, he feels that things have again come right, that Italy has indeed become "beautiful, courteous, lovable, as of old" (111).

Though Philip now discerns that Monteriano represents truths unknown in Sawston, he is not yet prepared to act upon his knowledge. As Caroline Abbott divines and as he admits, life for him is a spectacle with transfiguring moments. But for her an aesthetic view of life is not enough. She finds that Philip lacks commitment and the capacity to act, much as she admires his wisdom and understanding. Italy has reoriented her, and she becomes an oracle that gives Philip knowledge of himself. After their conversation in the church of Santa Deodata, the center of Monteriano's spiritual life, Philip not only admits that she is right about his irresolution but he also begins to love her, even though in Sawston he had thought her an uninteresting and unattractive woman. Philip in his regenerate phase leaves behind his passivity. Though he did not intervene in time to prevent Harriet from kidnapping the baby, he acts decisively in confessing the baby's death to Gino. After he tells Gino of the catastrophe, Philip is unprepared for a brutality that is as much Gino's birthright as his geniality. At the time of his reconciliation with Italy, Philip had again overestimated her glamor and forgotten that sordidness, violence, and primitive passion are realities as true now of Italian life as they had ever been.

Throughout his second sojourn in Italy Philip extends his knowledge of life. He realizes, for example, that all have contributed to the death of Gino's child. Even Gino, we can infer, set in motion the wheels of his own destruction by sending postcards to the baby's half-sister in England, thereby antagonizing the Herritons. Nor has Caroline in her benevolence been selfless. Yet Philip feels that only he has been trivial and cowardly, and he realizes that his own role in the senseless tragedy has been crucial. In his enlightenment he now sees that Italy combines all facets of experience into a dynamic synthesis. She does not evade the violent, the evil, and the sinister; but, in confronting them honestly, she negates their influence in favor of the good, the beautiful, and the true.

Closer contact with Caroline makes Philip's transformation complete. He can now believe that greatness is possible, as he regards her transfigured countenance: "Her eyes were open, full of infinite pity and full of majesty, as if they discerned the boundaries of sorrow, and saw unimaginable tracts beyond. Such eyes he had seen in great pictures but never in a mortal" (173). A timid rebel has become a goddess who sees beyond good and evil to the region of the eternal verities and who commands others by virtue of what she is. In the baby-bathing sequence she achieves beauty and serenity, this time not of a pagan goddess but of the Virgin Mary, becoming for Philip "to all intents and purposes, the Virgin and Child, with Donor" (141). As a goddess who has attained an infallible wisdom, she is Pallas Athena; as a goddess who hopelessly loves a man separated from her by impossible social barriers, she is Semele forever divided from a mortal, Endymion, whom she loves.[11] Philip's future existence in England may once again be humdrum, but he now sees life critically and in its full integrity: the result will be that he will no longer accept his mother and her values as sacrosanct. Now Sawston will never claim his undivided loyalty, nor will it claim Caroline's. Imagination has ennobled both of them.

Caroline Abbott undergoes vacillations similar to Philip's, although she has from the beginning more self-possession. Possibly because of her uncertainties, she becomes, as one critic has said, the most "surprising" and "touching" of Forster's "guardian" figures[12]—people whose intuitive wisdom guides others. Before the trip with Lilia, Caroline had impressed Philip as respectable rather than vital, but in Italy she had a moment of liberation when she encouraged Lilia, in revolt against Sawston, to marry Gino. She had awakened on this visit to "beauty and splendor," so much so that she alone, of all the women he had ever known, had seemed to Gino to be *simpatico*. Thus Gino tacitly admits that he and Caroline have affinities which, under favorable circumstances, might have reached fruition in the sexual bond. But Italy's challenge to Caroline's sensibilities on this first visit has not been deep enough to change her basically.

On her second trip to Italy Caroline reveals at first a single-minded intention to get control of Gino's child; she agrees with Harriet that Gino has no sense of sin and that he "murdered" Lilia. While she talks to Philip, she strokes the outlines of a Gothic window and, in so doing, becomes physically identified with one of Monteriano's manifestations of the spirit, its architecture. An inner liberation begins as her humane instincts assert themselves and take her further than her conscious ideas would sanction. The Italy of tradition has begun its mellowing effect on her, as on Philip; for it is by this window, as they look at the towers opposite, that they achieve their first real understanding. She attains more exalted emotion still after she attends the performance of *Lucia*, but then becomes ashamed of herself and asserts once more her intention of continuing at Monteriano "to champion morality and purity, and the holy life of an English home" (124). But in her dreams that night, music and beauty and laughter unsettle her; and Poggibonsi, the town traditionally antagonistic to Monteriano, becomes for her, like Sawston, "a joyless, straggling place, full of people who pretended" (125). Seeing Sawston now for what it is, how can she be other than a half-hearted defender of its values?

Both Philip and Caroline are educated to the intricacies of life and are no longer content with the simplifications of experience that satisfy the inhabitants of Sawston. Even before his first mission, the Italy of romance had been disillusioning for Philip, principally because Lilia intended to marry a dentist's son. A painful *éclaircissement* follows because false romance "which cannot resist the unexpected and the incongruous and the grotesque" (27) departs forever from him. For Italy teaches him that melodrama is possible, that experience can be lurid, exaggerated, and unpredictable, and that vital spiritual revelations have nothing to do with pleasing illusions.

The towers that dominate the skyline of Monteriano dominate the spiritual landscape of the novel. Many of the towers are broken (only seventeen of the original fifty-two remain), signifying that modern Italy may lack the full integration of powers that characterized her during the Middle Ages and the Renaissance. In comparison to Sawston, Italy still retains a sense of the complexities of experience; and the towers emphasize this truth. They look skyward but have their feet in the earth. They connote aspiration in their upward reaches; they convey mundane experience at their bases (advertisements often placard them); and they reach in their foundations toward the nether regions. If, as Philip says, the tower opposite "reaches up to heaven and down to the other place" and is thereby "a symbol of the town" (113), tower and town both signify the elusive complications of Italy and, by extension, of human life itself. They also symbolize to Lilia in their moonlit beauty a freedom that her frustrating marriage to Gino has denied her. In Philip's first view of them they are lit by the rays of the declining sun and become emblems of Italy's magical essence. They contribute, moreover, to the insubstantial aspect of Monteriano viewed from a distance, the towers then becoming masts for "some fantastic ship city of a dream" (27).

The other characters in the novel do not develop, either because they do not respond to the influence of Italy or because they encapsulate its influence (Gino). Harriet is inflexible and unchanging, "the same in Italy as in England—changing her disposition never, and her atmosphere under protest" (114). A similar uniformity characterizes Lilia, Mrs. Herriton, and Gino, all of whom impress us by what they are rather than by what they become. Like Harriet, who is "acrid, indissoluble, large," they register as commanding presences rather than as subtly envisioned personalities. They are monolithic in the singleness of their energies and in the concentration of their purposes; even Lilia, with her frivolity and irresponsibility, has her own intensity. All these individuals attain a stature convincing in its own terms, the strength that is to be associated with caricature (Harriet and Mrs. Herriton), or with an easygoing normality (Gino and Lilia), or with a primal vital force (Gino).

Gino is complex to the degree that the Italy he represents is a culture whose qualities resist easy definition. He is paradoxical and inconsistent rather than subtle, and the culture that he represents has determined his attributes. No more than Lilia or Harriet is he capable of self-criticism and the intelligent analysis of his own motives. Gino's excessive concern with the proprieties that his wife must observe provides even an unexpected link between him and the typical residents of Sawston, different as he is from the English middle class in most other respects. He is content to exploit the double standard of sexual morality; and he lacks any consciousness of the incongruities of his own actions. He cannot realize that his situation is national as well as personal, "that generations of ancestors, good, bad, or indifferent, forbade the Latin man to be chivalrous to the northern woman, the northern woman to forgive the Latin man" (65).

Gino's responses are instinctive rather than intellectual, despite his surface familiarity with Dante. Accordingly, he is both violent and magnanimous, vindictive and open-hearted. He can also, upon occasion, approach the demonic. His silent and explosive laughter when Philip accosts him; his stalking of Lilia, suggesting the actions of an enraged animal, when she threatens to cut off her money; and the depth of his anger and his sadistic torturing of Philip at the end of the novel all indicate his fiendish, uncontrolled, and uncontrollable aspect. To the intruding Caroline Abbott, Gino's smoke rings seem like a veritable breath from the pit.

But this hint of the demonic also provides a measure for the depths of life to be found in him. Gino thinks not only in terms of gratifying his animal impulses but of their relationship to the larger history of the race: he sees his son as the only sure guarantee of his own immortality (and Italy's). He has his unexpected generosities also. He not only forgives Philip but perjures himself for his benefit at the inquest over the baby's death, though Harriet may not be worth this conspiracy to save her reputation. He has sure intuitions when his affections are involved, and he penetrates to the very depths of his friend's nature: in the future, "he would pull out Philip's life, turn it inside out, remodel it, and advise him how to use it for the best" (174). As a real person, Gino is somewhat less convincing than the other characters because Forster has analyzed him less and has shown him less often in action. He may not be intellectual enough to be fully representative of Italian culture and to be an archetypal figure in this respect. His depths are emotional, not intellectual. To the extent that he symbolizes Italy, there are some dimensions of this country that he does not adequately mirror. But as an archetypal personification of elemental man he is more than adequate.

Where Angels Fear to Tread is a subtle, complex, and refreshing novel; and, in its total impact, it justifies the opinion that Forster from the first was an artist of maturity and power. The majority of his short stories also date from this period, and in them the romance elements of his universe predominate. In them the characters obtain some knowledge of themselves and the quality of their past lives through intuitive and visionary means. These experiences reorient these individuals, even if some of them are unable to turn their visions to account.

Forster's "Natural Supernaturalism": The Early Tales

The tales are almost all deft, sometimes self-conscious ventures into fantasy, a mode which Forster used intermittently in his novels. His novels are almost as much romance as realism; and fantasy could be regarded as romance in which the element of realism is even more in abeyance than it is in the novels. Yet Forster did his best work in his tales at the point where realism and fantasy merge. Such a fusion of the here and now with the intimations of the imagination Forster found in Lewis Carroll: ". . . fantasy slides into daily life, everyday life into fantasy, without a jerk, without the waving of a wand." [13] The finest tales illustrate this skilled fusion of realism and fantasy, but the weaker ones do not always attain it.

In "Mr. Andrews," "Co-ordination," "The Curate's Friend," and "The Rock" [14] Forster failed to dramatize conclusively his complex and original concepts. These tales tend to be patent allegories and, as a result, to lack substance and weight. His tendency in them—to rely almost totally upon fantasy—provides only tentative support for the values that he attempts to establish through personality and incident. Actual substance in "The Other Side of the Hedge" is also slighter than animating idea. The theme—that few men are willing to embrace a spirited self-sufficiency—is more challenging in the abstract than it is memorably embodied in Forster's parable. In "The Purple Envelope," which is in part social comedy, fantasy is only imperfectly assimilated into the tale's substance.

"The Machine Stops" is the only one of Forster's pure fantasies that is successful. Forster uses the conventions of science fiction in imagining a transformed society in the future, but he also uses them to protest against the depersonalizing dominion of the machine. Kuno is tragic because he hopes in vain for personal experience and a subjective fulfillment in a materialistic "Utopia." Mechanical efficiency overreaches itself in the tale, however; the artificial society disintegrates when "the machine stops." At their death, Kuno and his mother Vashti weep for dying mankind and its wasted possibilities. Forster achieved power in the tale through his ability to concentrate his energies and to achieve structural tautness. Some commentators have accorded "The Celestial Omnibus" high status, but one can maintain that here fantasy is imperfectly ballasted with the real, so that the boy's heroic ventures into heaven and the defeat of the snobbish Bons are at once too arbitrary and too sketchily conveyed. While "The Machine Stops" possesses an overplus of fantasy, a more modest story, "Ansell," probably contains as little overt fantasy as is possible in a Forster story, though the first-person narrator achieves intuitively an illumination as to the worthlessness of his academic career in contrast to a possible extended relationship with the farm boy, Ansell.

"Albergo Empedocle," "Other Kingdom," and "The Story of a Panic" are more authentic weldings of the realistic and the supernatural. Realistic detail, as a result, secures credence when Forster departs from the empirically verifiable—that is, when he resorts to fantasy. Forster's use of a narrator who is a minor character is an interesting and, on the whole, successful technical innovation in the stories. In "Albergo Empedocle" the narrator is wiser than the other people and functions as an embodiment of authorial value. In the other two stories he is obtuse, and his simplicity or imperceptiveness prevents him from reaching a sure assessment of experience. In either case, there exists a positive or a negative disjunction between the narrator's quality of mind and the events and characters that he comments upon.

"Albergo Empedocle" is an excellent story that remained uncollected until after Forster's death because of a publisher's decision and possibly because of its implied homosexual theme. The antagonists, Harold and Mildred Peaslake (his fiancée), lock in a deep-reaching conflict. Though Harold seems superficial and passive so long as he is under Mildred's domination, he possesses forces too powerful for her to control, even if they are not firm enough for him to be able to transform his contemporary society and to take a vital place in it. Instead of retreating to the greenwood as Maurice and Alec Scudder do in *Maurice*, Harold retreats to a happier civilization in the past—that of Greece where he had lived "differently," though to his imperceptive acquaintances he now seems sad. The narrator demonstrates Harold's superiority, though he himself had failed to respond to a personal call when Harold, before his onset of "madness," had asked him to come to Greece. Sympathy awakens for Harold, because the modern world makes of him a martyr when he rejects, after his vision of his anterior existence, Mildred and her assertive values.

"Other Kingdom" obliquely analyzes the effects produced by a conventional, ruthless man, Harcourt Worters, upon his sensitive, elfin fiancée, Evelyn Beaumont. The painfulness of her suffering intensifies after marriage, so that her escape from him is foreordained, and the extremity of her metamorphosis into a dryad, inhabiting one of her beloved trees, is justifiable. By this transformation Forster gains peace for Evelyn and suitable justice for a relentless husband—the loss of one whom he appreciates only as an object and not as a spirit. He is the antithesis of the self-sufficient Ford (Evelyn's friend), whose insight is as unerring as his human sympathy is complete.

"The Story of a Panic" develops a similar contrast between the conventional and the spontaneous, but this time one individual, Eustace, confronts a group of imperceptive people. One of these, the narrator, is aggravated by the unusual events that he must recount but cannot comprehend. The superiority of Eustace to the other English with him at Ravello is implied when he alone does not panic as a "catspaw" of wind, betokening the arrival of Pan, blows upon them at an upland picnic. He acknowledges in a flash of vision the god who stirs the deepest currents of his soul, and a bit later he rapturously praises all the forms and forces of nature. Gennaro, who, Judas-like, betrays

Eustace to his English guardians for silver, later dies like Christ for his friend when the English try to prevent Eustace's escape from confinement in the hotel—escape from constricted modern life to a free existence with the great god Pan.

In "The Road from Colonus," "The Eternal Moment," "Ralph and Tony," "The Story of the Siren," and "The Point of It" Forster combined, more successfully still, the actual with the purely imaginative; and he achieved an increased degree of credence for these works. The romance elements in them register more decisively when there is this interplay between realism and fantasy.

In "The Road from Colonus," the most haunting and powerful of all the tales, Forster uses myth ironically and satirically to give his story amplitude. Mr. Lucas just misses the tragic stature of a dying Oedipus through the officiousness of his daughter and survives to a querulous instead of a dignified old age. Ethel Lucas is an Antigone-like guardian of her father, but she is concerned only for his physical well-being, not for his soul. Toward the end of a discouraging expedition in Greece, Mr. Lucas visits a huge votive tree, inside whose hollow trunk he feels his soul expand, as he gazes upon the seemingly redemptive stream flowing through it. He experiences a kinship with the timeless energies of nature; and, in this moment of vision, he discovers the truth not only about Greece but about England and the whole of life.

From this supreme moment of transfiguration his daughter drags him away. As it turns out, that same night during a storm the votive tree fell upon the inn in which he had wished to stay, killing all the people it it. Mr. Lucas's later desiccation in London, the result of his apathetic existence, is more terrible by far than certain death would have been, had he been able to stay in rural Greece as he had wished. The inner life, Forster implies, reaches a maximum fullness, as it did for Mr. Lucas in the grove of plane trees; and it disintegrates thereafter if sustenance is denied it. Unless we are free to revive the precious visionary moment, or strong enough to remember it, it will perish as if it had never been.

In "The Eternal Moment" Forster enlarges upon the moral power exerted by the "symbolic moment" and the parlous effects that may follow its denial. A successful novelist, Miss Raby, finally faces the truth about herself, though this act disrupts the security she might have enjoyed in her last years. She perceives that her rejection of sex meant deterioration for a man who then dedicated himself to money instead of love. Thus she discovers two truths: our actions have infinite consequences, and the moment is eternal only for those with courage, foresight, and force enough to grasp it. She has had the strength to cherish the moment in memory; and from its transfiguring influence all that is worthwhile for her derived, at the same time that she may have missed the best in life by playing the shocked lady when a boy had been on fire with love for her. She feels, however, that she has lived consistently and "worthily," even if she has never known completeness of being. The mythological and fantastic are in abeyance in this tale except as Forster's imagination raises to its true—and greater than normal—proportions a significant incident from Miss Raby's past.

In another haunting and powerful story, "Ralph and Tony" (published in *Arctic Summer and Other Fiction* in 1980 but dating from 1903) Forster centered the romance and mythic elements in only one character, the medical student Tony who, on holiday among his beloved mountains, becomes an archetypal presence, a "radiant demigod who had seen into heaven." Forster never tried to publish the story and never mentioned it to his friends, possibly because Ralph Holme and his mother may have resembled too closely Forster and his mother.

In the story Forster dramatizes the disruptive effects of the primitive forces found in Tony's nature upon the "civilized" Ralph. Despite his free disposition, Tony is rather conventional and reacts with active contempt toward Ralph whom he regards as "decadent." Somewhat ambiguously, Ralph feels attraction to both Tony and his sister, Margaret; and he suggests to Tony that he marry Margaret and live with both of them. Tony is outraged, especially when Ralph becomes emotional and pleads with him; beside himself with anger, Tony savagely kicks the prostrate Ralph. Ralph then tries to climb the mountain that he calls "Justice," feeling that he must survive such a test as this. Tony rescues him when he persists in this dangerous enterprise. As for Tony, his strenuous exertions exacerbate a latent heart condition and cause him to fall when he is carrying Ralph to safety. Though he will continue to live, Tony must give up the soul-expanding mountains, even the visiting of them, because of the altitude.

At the story's end, the men achieve some sort of understanding, with Tony apparently willing to accept Ralph's marriage. Does Tony save the life of a man whom he hates or of a man whom he unconsciously loves? Is the violence toward Ralph a covert form of sexual expression? In any case, Ralph seems to love Tony more intensely than the woman he wishes to marry. Largeness of spirit and momentary vindictiveness can coexist in an untamed man like Tony, who heralds the Stephen Wonham of *The Longest Journey*. Moreover, the deprivations caused by the physical collapse are tragic for an individual like Tony whose capacious soul demands active expression. Tony's weak heart, in effect, condemns him to a living death in a society that stresses appearances and refuses to acknowledge the realities of human nature. And in such a society it is impossible for an effete man like Ralph ever to attain wholeness.

Myth and fantasy are primary elements in "The Story of the Siren." The Sicilian boy who tells about the Siren has a scapegrace brother, a kind of devil's disciple who alone in the village sees the Siren and becomes unsettled as a result of this confrontation with naked reality. His wife goes mad after her encounter with the Siren. The child to be born to them, it is rumored, will be Antichrist, and will raise up the Siren and restore the world. Accordingly, a Christian priest, acting from a fear that is not Christian, pushes the woman from a cliff before her son can be born. The Christian community that concurs in the priest's deed fails to see that perhaps the greatest sin is to do evil that good may supposedly result. By her equanimity the Siren implicitly condemns human fears and hatreds and the village's lack of Christian charity. When the Siren will rise, the baleful power of all restrictive conventions will end; and she will "sing, destroy silence, primness, and cruelty, and save the world." [15] The source of much of the story's strength is the implication that the Siren is to be equated with a moral reality that transcends good and evil. She symbolizes, therefore, the difficult truth that men must face if they are to be wholly free. Thus mythology in the story serves metaphysical as well as purely aesthetic ends.

"The Point of It" is as noteworthy for the rendition of ideas central in Forster as it is for establishing a credible supernatural atmosphere. In the first scene, Micky is guarding his friend Harold, who has been sent to the seaside to recuperate from overexertion. Alarmed at Harold's frenzied rowing, Micky confesses that he does not quite see the point of such effort. Harold replies that Micky some day will see "the point of it" and forthwith dies from an overstrained heart. The twofold point eludes Micky for some fifty years: his own life never reached a higher intensity than in Harold's company, and Harold—in precipitate yielding to instinct—had achieved an even more exalted ecstasy, which opened out for him the utmost possibilities to be reached by the self. Until the final moment of the tale, Micky fails to attain the truths that he had once almost grasped, that intuition is superior to the unaided intellect and that one must be pure in heart to grasp the beatific vision. This short "life-in-life" sequence at the seacoast is succeeded by a longer sequence recounting Mickey's death-in-life as a prosperous, smug civil servant. He dies violently when he intervenes in a quarrel between two slum women, and then becomes a denizen on a plain in a Dantean hell, where he undergoes a death-in-death experience. But he becomes aware of his faults and is thereby prepared for redemption.

Micky's conversion follows. A spirit—no doubt Harold or his ghost—now comes to disturb the apathetic dwellers beyond the river Acheron by its singing. Of the shades in Hell Micky is the only one to be influenced by this Unseen Presence because he alone wishes to remember his ignoble past with a view to reordering it. He now arrives at a phase of life-in-death in which he learns that the ultimate reality resides in the sheer desire for strength and beauty. Mickey's second "death" occurs—his being born into Eternity—and it is accompanied by terrible pain as he faces the reality that he had previously disregarded. Once Mickey says that he desires light, the counseling spirit vanishes, and he finds himself back in the boat where he had been years ago with Harold. Micky has at last found "the point of it"—as Harold had promised he would—that a man can save himself only by a desire to retain, or to reach, spiritual purity and ecstasy. The reverberations of significance in the story demonstrate Forster's intrepid fusion of social commentary and aesthetic inventiveness. This union of the critically acute and the imaginatively ingenious is, in fact, the chief excellence of Forster's short stories, as it also tends to be of his novels.

Chapter Three

"The Union of Shadow and Adamant": *The Longest Journey*

Rickie Elliot and the Life of the Imagination

The Longest Journey is the most elusive of Forster's novels and one of the most difficult to assess. If one judges it in terms of the qualities customarily associated with realism in literature—probability of motive and incident, an evenness in the texture of writing appropriate to a factual re-creation of milieu, a sparseness in the symbolic dimensions of the narrative, and a primary emphasis upon the characters in their usual appearances rather than as archetypes—he will tend to regard *Journey* negatively. The novel, besides, is not entirely free of inconsistencies and structural weaknesses. On the credit side, we find striking merits, many of them to be associated with the romance conventions that Forster's fiction consistently illustrates, though he is adept, as we have seen, in combining romance with social realism, often in the form of domestic comedy or of the comedy of manners. Among the distinctive qualities of *Journey* are a brisk narrative pace, a poetic yet precise style, a piquant humor, an unusual angle of vision, an eloquent descriptive power, an evocative symbolism, an elemental quality in the people and the action, a sensibility alive to the tragic nuances of human existence, and a sure sense, frequently, of psychological motivation. Rickie Elliot, the protagonist, is both the man who is severely tried and educated by the social milieu of which he is part and the quest figure in search of the truth that will illuminate. Both as a representative man in his society and as an archetypal presence, Rickie is interesting and often compelling, and most of the other chief characters in the novel have this same double dimension.

In 1904 Forster first conceived the idea of writing a book about a man with an illegitimate half-brother.[1] Forster's experiences in Wiltshire were to give this subject focus and intensity: he talked with shepherds there who suggested the character of Stephen Wonham (the illegitimate half-brother to Rickie Elliot), and he appreciated the beauty and the mystery of the ancient Figsbury Rings, the original of the Cadbury Rings in the novel.[2] Forster's defining in retrospect the subjects that he wished to incorporate into this novel suggests at once its richness, its diffuseness, and its perhaps overambitious scope: "There was the metaphysical idea of Reality ('the cow is there'): there was the ethical idea that reality must be faced (Rickie won't face Stephen); there was the idea, or ideal, of the British Public School; there was the title, exhorting us in the words of Shelley not to love one person only; there was Cambridge, there was Wiltshire."[3] Each of the themes that Forster mentions in this passage we shall consider at least in passing.

Forster further accounted for the imaginative power exerted in the book when he confessed that Rickie Elliot is his most autobiographical character.[4] The solicitude with which he analyzed Rickie and his retreat from the light reveals Forster's own identification with him. Rickie may see certain aspects of reality with less clarity than do some other characters, but he arouses our interest more consistently, since, as one critic explains, he tries to do more by assimilating the best features of several approaches to life.[5] He is, besides, fallibly human; and his mistakes derive from frailty, not viciousness of nature. The equanimity and justice of his standards compel even his hostile aunt, Emily Failing, to admit that he is the true heir of her deceased husband, Tony, the wisest character in the novel, even though he figures in it only as a voice from the dead and was sometimes ineffectual when he was alive.

Like the other humanists in the novel (his friend Stewart Ansell, his teaching colleague Jackson, and his dead uncle Tony Failing), Rickie continually tries to define for himself the nature of ultimate truth, although his quest may never be completed. To his detriment, he distrusts the concrete as opposed to an idealizing of it. Rickie's romantic imagination provides his greatest strength and weakness; his initial values are not so much mistaken as seen too often in faulty perspective. He is, furthermore, subject to attack by people more masterful than he; and he does not always know how, therefore, to hold fast to the best of his perceptions. Through Rickie, Forster projects the beauties and potential rewards of the imaginative life, and, even more insistently, its potential dangers for an uncritical temperament.

Because Rickie would rather examine his own mind than argue in support of ideas, he does not participate actively in the opening discussion by a group of Cambridge University undergraduates on the nature of reality: whether "the cow" is objectively out there or genuine only as the mind refracts it. He is too diffident, possibly too skeptical, to have formed definite views about the "reality" of the cow; at the same time, he is too poetical by instinct to do much with pure logic. He senses that reality is neither so "ideal" as Tilliard insists nor so solid as Stewart Ansell maintains. Rather, Rickie feels that elms are neither solid objects, independent of the individual's sensibility, nor insubstantial phenomena, lurking only at the borders of our minds. He believes that elms may be dryads, and he develops for himself a reality at once concrete and ideal but one that is weighted too greatly toward the ideal, though Forster admits that "the line between the two is subtler than we admit." [6] But judging by the ultimate and posthumous success of his stories, Rickie's imaginativeness and his poetic intuitions are positive attributes if, in an excessive degree, they are limiting ones.

The opening chapter through Ansell is a confirmation of the "realism" of G. E. Moore and a protest against "idealistic" modes of interpreting experience, modes which stress the element of subjective perception as providing the sole clue to our understanding of reality. [7] The road to the other world, the intangible and the mystical, is through the objectively discriminated entities of this world; or their reality is not to be denied. Forster has some elements of Romanticism in his temper, and the Romantics often stressed a subjective or idealistic mode of apprehending our experience. In his direct approach to, and communication with, the intangible, Forster has affinities with idealistic philosophers such as, for example, Plotinus, the romantic pantheists, and oriental religionists; but basically, he is in accord with another aspect of Romanticism that regards the realities of the visible world as indispensable if one is to penetrate to a transcendental realm.

In the main, Forster begins with, and returns to, a stress upon the solid existence of the objects that surround us. Moore did not, in fact, deny the reality of the mystical, but felt that the subjective or idealistic view of the world was suspect when it denied the objective validity of the world outside ourselves. Certainly Forster, in characters like Rickie Elliot of *Journey* and Helen Schlegel of *Howards End*, would stress the nefarious effects of an unballasted subjectivity. In *Journey* Forster is also critical of any form of action that would deny the facts of our social lives and that would evade the disconcerting and unpleasant aspects of life by resort to comforting illusions. Such "idealism," of course, motivates the behavior of Agnes and Herbert Pembroke, and of Mr. Elliot and his sister, Mrs. Failing. Chapter 28, which is author commentary at the end of the second movement ("Sawston"), balances the opening discussion of the nature of reality in the first chapter of the first movement ("Cambridge"). In his later comments Forster emphasizes the pernicious effects of an imagination that departs radically from the truth inherent in the basic, tangible facets of experience: "Will it really profit us so much if we save our souls and lose the whole world?" (246).

Visitors for Rickie—Agnes Pembroke and her brother Herbert—interrupt the discussion in Chapter 1. Ansell, who is the enemy of "the ideal," regards Agnes as unreal because he detects intuitively that her life is built upon illusion; and he refuses to greet her, since, according to his standards, she does not even exist. Later, he criticizes her as being neither serious nor truthful. Shortly after the visit, Agnes's lover, Gerald Dawes, dies in a football match; and she turns for comfort to Rickie. Love develops, and over Ansell's protest, which is in some part homosexual jealousy, Rickie marries Agnes. He has

elected to pursue "the longest journey" in the company of one
person, a course of conduct about which Shelley, in a passage
from "Epipsychidion" quoted in the novel (138), is skeptical.
By so doing, Rickie sacrifices his friends and his genuine
interests, the capacity to grow and develop intellectually and
spiritually. Physically, Rickie is no match for the overbearing,
now dead Gerald; and he fails to dominate his wife. In turn,
Agnes is selfish, unimaginative, and materialistic.

Rickie is also false to his deepest self when, in order to marry
quickly, he leaves Cambridge to go as teacher to Sawston
School, where he adopts Herbert's standards; and somewhat
later in Wiltshire, he is once more false to his basic nature
when, at Agnes's behest, he denies the claims upon him of his
half-brother, Stephen Wonham. Mrs. Failing had revealed to
Rickie, in a moment of pique at the center of the Cadbury
Rings, the identity of Stephen, when Rickie and Agnes were
visiting her at Cadover House in Wiltshire. Rickie then
assumes that Stephen is the bastard child of his hated father.
Not until Rickie marries and Mrs. Failing expels Stephen from
Cadover, does he learn, through Ansell, that Stephen is his
mother's illegitimate son. Mrs. Elliot had been the victim of
her husband's cruelty and had turned to Robert, a Wiltshire
farmer and man of the earth, for release. The lovers eloped to
Sweden, where Stephen was conceived and Robert was
drowned immediately thereafter. When Mrs. Elliot had no
option other than to return to her hated husband, Stephen
became the adopted child of the Failings.

Once Rickie learns the full truth about Stephen, he has the
courage to repudiate Agnes and to join him. But Stephen will
tolerate him only if Rickie accepts him as a man, not as a
symbol: "Here am I and there are you" (262). On a journey
back to Wiltshire, the two reach a deep accord when they sail
flame boats down a stream near Cadover House. A chance
occurrence shatters this harmony, when Stephen breaks his
promise to Rickie not to drink. Rickie comes upon his drunken
brother just in time to rescue him at the local crossing but dies
when he fails to escape the oncoming train. After Rickie's
death, Stephen marries and cherishes his brother's memory by
calling his child after their mother; and he also acknowledges

that Rickie's money has made possible his free life upon the beloved Wiltshire acres. When Stephen sacramentally names his child after her grandmother, he, in effect, makes whole the photograph of his mother which he had torn in impatience with Rickie for regarding him as the symbolic descendant of their mother rather than as the vital man that he is.

Rickie starts with a truth which he later fails to observe but to which still later he returns. Metaphysical finality derives from the coloring given to our perceptions by the modulating reason—or the disciplined imagination—not from the exclusive exercise of either senses or intellect. The most illuminating glimpses of the truth, then, depart from a strict empiricism, even if one must never depart completely from it; and Rickie realizes that imagination must transform the world of sensation for that world to achieve fullness of meaning, though he does not yet realize that the imagination can also mislead. But the disciplined imagination elicits, or reinforces, the innermost significances latent in the objects that we come to know.

The reality inheres in concretions, but its furthest ramifications are visionary and to be grasped only intermittently. Furthermore, it can never be fully defined or exhausted. Ansell's quaint exercise in the concentric patterning of squares and circles—fashioning each time "a new symbol for the universe, a fresh circle within the square" (199)—now gathers new meaning. If, as he maintains, the figure farthest inside is the real one, its outlines lose identity as its significance intensifies. Accordingly, final reality is as difficult to perceive as it is to pinpoint. As one of Forster's best critics, George H. Thomson, asserts, the inmost figure is the circle; and it links with the other circle images such as the Cadbury Rings and the dome of the British Museum where Ansell studies.[8] All these images act as expansive symbols. The most commonplace object, in fact, may open out to proclaim that the infinite lies within it. This is partly the significance of Ansell's striking matches when the cow's substantial or ideal nature is in question. The brands of wood are symbols of an actuality in the here and now, but, lit with flame, these actualities bear deep within them an irradiating essence that cannot be measured with exactness. Fire is a symbol of this innermost, transfiguring reality and dominates

the haunting sequence toward the end of the novel wherein the
boys sail flame boats through the arches of a bridge. The paper
balls, lit by Stephen into mystic roses of flame, are emblematic
of the infinite emanating from, yet situated deep within, the
natural. Rickie loses sight of his flaming rose before Stephen
does; the overspreading life-force will die out from him, we
infer, but it will be preserved through Stephen's children.

In the end, the imagination that allows Rickie to achieve so
much misleads him. So, after Gerald's death, Agnes becomes
for Rickie, in Ansell's view, "a single peg" upon which to hang
"all the world's beauty" (87). Rickie sees her, as if with the
vision of Blake, "a virgin widow, tall, veiled, consecrated"
(64); for him, she becomes a transcendent being, a Beatrice, a
Clara Middleton, a Brunhilde, "a light . . . suddenly held
behind the world" (90) to illuminate his existence. The light
she effuses, however, is not warm and life-enhancing; it is, as
Widdrington (another of Rickie's Cambridge friends) says, the
brisk glare induced when an electric light clicks on. In practice,
Rickie's idealism flourishes at the expense of his sense of fact.
Tragically for him, he falls in love "through the imagination"
rather than "through the desires." A vision, we conclude, can
falsify as well as illuminate. So Agnes's imposing beauty and
brusque good nature conceal a philistinism and a vindictiveness; and when, finally, Rickie sees her for what she is, his
life with her seems as unreal as the grotesque sheep engraved
upon their domestic accounts book. At this point "the cow" is
no longer "there" for him. Because Agnes leads him away
from his true moral bent and prevents him from acknowledging Stephen, she is also the Eve to Rickie's Adam, while Mrs.
Failing is her satanic accomplice.[9]

Like her brother Herbert, Agnes slays imagination. Only
"the great world" is significant for her; and she is at enmity
with Ansell's intellectual distinction, with Rickie's creative
expansiveness, and with Stephen's natural beauty and spontaneous morality: "Actual life might seem to her so real that
she could not detect the union of shadow and adamant that
men call poetry" (154). Foreign to her is that valid sort of
empiricism—a sacramental sense of the actual—which all three
men at various times reveal. Because she is incapable of grasp-

ing the essence of what she perceives, she falsifies reality more than Rickie does, who has been too eager to transform the actual into his heart's desire. His notion of Stephen as hero is stereotypical, and he is unable, with consistency, to penetrate his brother's ruffianly exterior to his genuine strength beneath.

Rickie is partly justified in his disgust with Stephen's drunkenness (he fears the desecration of Stephen's powerful organism and the tendency of the drunkard to resort to "secondhand" intensities); but he reacts too seriously, regarding the situation as a disastrous defeat for his vigorous ideals as to what other people should be. For Mrs. Failing, Rickie is associated with "the cracked bell" which sounds from Cadover Church. The bell sounds as she tells him in the Cadbury Rings about Stephen and again at Rickie's funeral as, with grim satisfaction, she denominates him a failure. The cracked bell signifies less his personal deficiencies and material failure—since he does prevail in his death and after—than his aborted career, his truncated development and influence, his deflection from wholeness, and his defeated aspirations.

Rickie Elliot: Perceptive and Misguided Humanist

For the most part, values in *The Longest Journey* are defined, explicitly or symbolically, through Rickie's sensibility, through his actions, through Forster's comments upon him, and through the other characters' views of him. In those parts not refracted through Rickie's consciousness, characters and incident ultimately impinge upon his fortunes. Perceptiveness and blindness in close conjunction make of Rickie one of the most enigmatic and complex characters in recent literature. His contradictory personality, his paradoxical ideas, his changing relationships with others, and the ironic disparities between his conduct and his inspiriting standards bring the book into focus and elicit from it varied chains of significance. Even at his most quixotic and weak, he inspires our interest, and we perceive that he is more than the outcast and failure he judges himself to be in moments of discouraged self-appraisal at Sawston School. As one critic says, he gains our sympathy because it is more difficult at times to endure convention, as

Rickie does, than to break with it.[10] Rickie is a sensitive individual who tries to live creatively in accordance with his humanistic and Christian values and who tries to explore different realms of experience with a view to reconciling them. He fails in doing so as a man of more than average insight, who makes an all but disastrous mistake, a wrong marriage.

Still, he is the valid hero of romance who is tested by ordeals in the three different milieus of which he is a part. He deserves approbation for a conscientious pursuit of truth wherever it may lead. He cherishes the intellectual values of Cambridge, as Ansell represents them, and also the firm (yet mystical) realities of nature, as Stephen embodies them; he aims for a synthesis of abstract and concrete, through the agency of imagination and purely personal values, much as Tony Failing, his uncle, tried to achieve before him. He would like to do so, while becoming part of the greater world of Sawston. In these attempts at social and philosophical integration Rickie fails because he is weaker than his insights, because he misjudges the strength of Sawston standards, because he attempts too much, and because he has less immediate wisdom in personal relationships than do Ansell and Stephen, for whom such relations are not so obsessive.

But, if Rickie succumbs to the enemy of the imagination, the philistine world of Sawston, his efforts to bridge the concrete and the transcendent and then to relate these realms of value to the larger world provide the framework upon which the most meaningful existence may be built. Rickie is deflected from attaining a vibrant synthesis, although his surviving influence enables Stephen to achieve, more fully, such a harmonizing of powers. Like a typical prophet, Rickie is sacrificed in the interest of the fuller life-to-be which he helps to bring about.

By the end of the novel he has managed to get free of the malevolent forces at Sawston and Cadover. Nevertheless, a certain ambiguity invests Rickie at the close. He defends himself eloquently against Mrs. Failing and her denial of the free life. Following his disillusion over Stephen's drunkenness and broken promise, however, he seems, in death, to have denied again the light and to have reverted to her views. Yet it is possible to feel that he has made his concession to his aunt—

that convention is truth—with only his conscious mind and that his deeper self achieves worthy expression in laying down his life for his brother and in writing the stories, composed before and after the Sawston experience, which win for him posthumous fame and for his brother financial security. He serves the earth even while he expresses disillusionment with it to his aunt as he dies.

In a standard essay on this novel, John Magnus finds in Rickie a Hermes analogue.[11] In classical mythology Hermes was Demeter's servant; in the novel Rickie helps Demeter (Mrs. Elliot) bring about Stephen's survival as a natural force, just as Hermes rescued Persephone in ancient lore from the underworld and enabled Demeter to bring back the spring. Magnus also equates Rickie with the Hermes of Praxiteles and Stephen with the child Dionysus under the god's protective care. We can carry this interpretation farther and see in Stephen himself "a divine child" like the Dionysus of the statue. It was as a child radiating light and serenity that the naked Stephen appeared to his uncle Tony Failing, long ago on the roof at Cadover house. As a divine child, Stephen is to become the savior of his race; and he develops into a man in whom are concentered all the most durable fibers of the English people. His child in turn becomes another such harbinger of the future.

Rickie's goodwill, generosity, and human insight derive from his mother, not from his father and aunt, who are negative and evil forces. Rickie remembers his father as more a monster than a man, as one whose eyes showed unkindness, cowardice, and fear, "as if the soul looked through dirty window-panes" (23), and whose voice was suave but whip-like. The leaden frames in Mr. Elliot's flower vases, like concealed and coiled sea serpents, are emblematic of the concealed and coiled venom in his nature. The image is linked with the snake-like stream of water that intrudes into Mrs. Failing's bower as she writes the memoir of her husband. This group of images suggests a Mephistophelean element in both brother and sister. In typical moments they express themselves through diabolical laughter. As for Mr. Elliot, he never gave himself, never did things for love, and he was, therefore, incapable of attaining the culture that most people credited him with possessing. He remained an inhumane aesthete. Despite his iconoclasm, he lacked the sincerity to be truly unconventional. Mrs. Failing is yet a more formidable and tenacious force than her brother and rightfully describes herself as a dragon, whose malevolent force the two protagonist figures, Rickie and Stephen, must negate.[12] She is in the main a fictional portrait of Forster's abrasive Uncle Willie (Forster), with perhaps some infusion of the peremptory Countess von Arnim, author of *Elizabeth of the German Garden*. His home, Acton House, in Northumbria, served as a model for Cadover in *Journey*.[13]

In Rickie, Forster embodied many of his humanistic—and Christian—values: kindness, consideration, tact, unselfishness, and sympathy. Since these qualities are largely Christian, it is no accident that Rickie belongs to the Anglican Church. At Cambridge, Rickie's lameness does not separate him from others, since his geniality, his enthusiasm, and his good nature—qualities nurtured in him by the university—allow him to regard his defect as the minor impediment it is. Until his denial of Stephen, Rickie reflects the genius of Cambridge which educates by indirection. He hopes, furthermore, that he will never be peevish or unkind; so long as he is in congenial surroundings he never falls from his standard. The set of Rickie's moral nature is indicated in Mrs. Failing's opinion of the half-brothers. She prefers Stephen's strength to Rickie's "blatant unselfishness"; but, in so doing, she tacitly admits Rickie's superior sensitivity and sympathy.

A sophisticated humanism enables Rickie likewise to defend convincingly the complex relationship existing between beauty and ethics. Agnes maintains that Rickie is "cracked" in his enthusiasm for the pictures inside the church at Madingley Hall at Cambridge. His concern is genuine in contrast to Agnes's superficial interest; and he reveals his aestheticism by maintaining that nothing beautiful is ever to be regretted. He feels, nevertheless, that beauty is only a means to the end of awareness and has little value if it does not lead to such enlargement. He admires his Uncle Tony for rejecting the arts that he loved, a "cultured paradise," for the end of securing "more decent people in the world" (188). In a quarrel with his aunt over the Church of England services at Cadover he refuses to admit that their tawdriness reflects adversely upon Christianity. Rather, he sees that a sense of beauty whose gratification is relentlessly pursued becomes sterile and inhuman. He remembers that his father had had perfect taste which made him seem all the more inhuman and inhumane.

With the Pembrokes, practicality reigns; they serve "the great world"; they assume that their souls are thereby nourished; and they fail to obtain mastery over conflicting imperatives because they refuse to recognize the existence of values opposed to their own. Thus Agnes is robust and practical, desires only a frank good-fellowship in marriage, and discourages intimacies based on emotion. Herbert is the spokesman at Sawston for a debasing pragmatism: the use of tradition where it avails, and the use of new departures where they avail. Such opportunism Tony Failing had repudiated; he had been interested in the practical life, but he felt that such a life could only be attained through dedication in part to ideal ends.

Like all of Forster's good humanists, Rickie attempts to reach some middle ground between the poles of permanence and change. At his best, he acknowledges the complexities of the moral life and tries to reconcile them. Although, in his quest for certitude, he fastens with excessive tenacity upon those elements in his experience that connote the permanent, he never completely loses his flexibility. His respect for the general, the philosophical, and the universal, moreover, enriches his mind, even if it may sometimes mislead him.

In his most lucid moments Rickie bridges in thought and conduct the gulf between the eternal and the transient. Thus, he finds that "the rough sea," the incessant flux of our ordinary existence, can only be restrained by the breakwaters that humanistic culture or religion build: the culture which, embodying racial wisdom, has transcended the wasting action of time, or the religion which, powerful in spirituality, has survived the passing centuries and has for its symbols in the novel the spire of Salisbury Cathedral or the towers of St. Mary's Roman Catholic Church at Cambridge. In the modern age, the sea's disintegrative currents have not lessened; but the accretions of permanently valuable knowledge mean that the human "bubbles" on these turbulent waters break less frequently than they did formerly.

Forces that result in a modicum of order must countervail those that lead to ceaseless change; otherwise, the individual's life will lack a sense of direction and purpose. A genuine stability, able to assimilate or to curb pressures from without, is absent from Dunwood House at Sawston School, despite continued recourse there to standardizing custom and convention. There, contact both with ordering principle and dynamic flux is missing: Dunwood House becomes an "unnecessary ship," lacking connection with the currents of change in the sea beneath or with the permanencies of the shore; and the sea it traverses is "frothy" and volatile, not "rough" and substantial. The ideal, especially in its interested and self-serving aspect, and not the real is supreme at the School; the abstract rather than the concrete, the institutional rather than the personal hold sway, so that after two years of teaching in this wasteland Rickie finds completely absent "personal contest, personal truces, personal love" (289).

That life is dynamic but has its core of permanent and ordered values is one truth implicit in the fascinating nature symbolism. In Wiltshire streams constantly carry water to the sea while a permanent substratum of chalk underlies them; the waters erode the surfaces of the chalk formations but leave untouched their central core. Orion and the other stars vary their appearances with the seasons but always return; the Cadbury Rings last as a monument over the centuries but eminences of ground like these act as a watershed to fill the running streams and will, in thousands of years, be worn down themselves. Intellectually, Rickie understands this dichotomy but in practice he tends to elevate some aspect of nature or some person into a rigid image and to deny the element of mutability in experience.[14]

Nature receives ambiguous emphasis in the novel. Whereas the earth confirms the spiritual largeness of Stephen and his father Robert, these men recognize that its influence is not always beneficent; and to Rickie, responsive to its beauties, the earth mostly seems cruel and relentless. Because of his experiences with Varden whom the other boys persecute for his large ears and because of the death of his own child, Rickie now "perceived more clearly the cruelty of Nature, to whom our refinement and piety are but as bubbles, hurrying downwards on the turbid waters" (208). Yet if nature is arbitrary, it is never petty nor other than commanding in its beauty and vitality.

When Forster describes Rickie as suffering from "the primal curse," the "knowledge of good-and-evil," he speaks ironically; for Rickie's knowledge is also a virtue. Rickie knows there are two sides to a question; he often sees the other side, to his immediate detriment. Comprehension of moral complexity characterizes subtly intelligent people like Rickie, who are in contrast to the unimaginative, falsely simplifying Pembrokes. Those who understand most things suffer most; the sensitive suffer for their sensitivity, as does Rickie in this novel. If full knowledge sometimes immobilizes him for positive action, it yet enables him to probe deeply into life so long as he is true to his best impulses. It is his tragedy that in practice his mind grows less supple, that at Sawston he becomes "the limpet" to Herbert's "whelk," and that he loses his sense of life as "good-and-evil" when he condones the absolutist standards of Sawston.

Structure in *The Longest Journey*: The Role of Persons and Places

The novel consists of three symphony-like movements, "Cambridge," "Sawston," and "Wiltshire"; and the tripartite structure emphasizes the crucial importance for Rickie of places and of the people who inhabit them. Forster also uses more intricately than in *Where Angels Fear to Tread* or *A Room with a View* the repeated image, with variations, to secure an incremental symbolic effect. In so doing, he heralds his practice in *Howards End* and *A Passage to India*. Examples of such recurring motifs are the following: Ansell's exercise of putting squares into constantly diminishing circles; flowing streams; chalk; Orion; Demeter; the Cadbury Rings; Salisbury Cathedral spire; Agnes as Medusa; the cow and its "reality"; Mrs. Elliot's voice from the dead; the railroad level-

crossing and the bridge eventually built there; the references to
Wagner in connection with Agnes and with the bridge and
water motifs; flame and fire; and the Madingley Dell. There is
no space to analyze fully all the recurring image clusters,
though a number of them figure incidentally in this discussion.

Ansell is Forster's spokesman at many points, and Forster
presents him sympathetically. The Cambridge of the novel is
the one that Forster knew at the beginning of the century, "the
Cambridge of G. E. Moore . . . the fearless uninfluential
Cambridge that sought for reality and cared for truth.
Ansell is the undergraduate high-priest of that local shrine,
Agnes Pembroke is its deadly debunker." [15] A. R. Ainsworth,
a devoted disciple of Moore, served Forster as model for
Ansell, but H. O. Meredith in a general way also contributed
to the portrait. [16] Ansell exemplifies the life of the intellect, but
he also sees the plain facts of existence more truthfully than
Rickie does. Ansell it is who rescues Rickie from the prison of a
marriage by exposing melodramatically his hypocrisy to the
assembled people at Sawston School and by causing him to face
the actuality of Stephen's existence as a brother and as the
illegitimate son of an adored mother. Under Ansell's tutelage
Rickie attains a new perspective when Ansell takes him "behind right and wrong, to a place where only one thing matters—that the Beloved should rise from the dead" (267), that
is, to a region where intuitions of truth are pristine and not
obstructed by social conventions, by prejudices, or by precon-
ceived ideas, to a region where Mrs. Elliot's affair with Robert
can be seen as transcendent passion, not as sinful excess. In
practice Ansell sometimes forgets that the individual is the
reality from whom all else derives. As Rickie sees, Ansell is
better at discussing love and death in the abstract than at
analyzing lovers and dying men. But by and large he is true to
his basic belief in the objective existence of men and natural
phenomena, and he is reinforced in his "realism" by the meeting with Stephen for whom people exist as such. Stephen's
hitting him with a clod of earth in the grounds of Dunwood
House, in effect, strengthens Ansell's sense of the solid reality
of all that surrounds him.

Ansell is not yet the true heir of the ancients but is acquiring by the end of the book fuller understanding of classical virtues and of ancient civilization with the knowledge imparted by Stephen and by the essays of Tony Failing. Though Ansell's grasp of the elemental is sronger than it has ever been, he also admits the need for the transcendent, in that "the holiness of the heart's imagination" (226) will alone enable him to classify and interpret facts with a minimum degree of distortion.

The second movement, "Sawston," dramatizes the corrupting influence of philistine England upon Rickie when, in order to marry Agnes, he consents to be a master at her brother's school. As its title would indicate, "Wiltshire," the third movement, emphasizes what Forster had previously hinted at, the redemptive influence of earth. Appropriately, the man who establishes the closest contact with the earth, Stephen's father Robert, figures for the first time; and we are taken to the past and the circumstances of his elopement with Mrs. Elliot. Again, as in the first movements of the novel, events involving Stephen prove decisive for Rickie. The flame boat episode in Chapter 23 is climactic in its assertion of the newfound unity between the brothers, whereas in Chapter 24 Stephen's broken promise to Rickie to desist from drinking separates them.

Through Stephen, Forster forcefully asserts the powers of earth over the spirit. Full rapport with the energies of nature implants in Stephen an elemental wisdom which enables him to discern pretentiousness of all kinds. For Stephen, people are real in themselves and not symbols. Accordingly, unlike Rickie, he will never undertake "the longest journey" in the company of one whom he has idealized: "love for one person was never to be the greatest thing he knew" (260). In spite of his lack of education, he has the intuitive insight of Forster's archetypal characters. Accordingly, in the epilogue he deflates Herbert Pembroke who, Stephen feels, has always been bounded by conventions and by the desire to "tidy" out of existence those who do not conform to them. Later, when Stephen sleeps out at night with his child, he ritualistically confirms his oneness with the earth. Instinctively identifying himself with the forces of continuity cherished by Forster, he knows that he has created life and that over the centuries men with his passions and thoughts will triumph in England.

Tony Failing had said that there is no such person as a Londoner: he is only a man fallen from the life-giving forces to be found in rural traditions. As a sign of his increased wisdom, Rickie likewise learns that towns are "excrescences" in which men lead purposeless lives. When the brothers return to Cadover, they are aware that the power of earth grows stronger as they leave Salisbury behind. The only ornament in Stephen's room at Cadover, a framed picture of the Demeter of Cnidus, indicates his affinity with this goddess of earth. The fact that the picture sways from a cord in the middle of his attic may signify that Demeter's influence over him is dynamic rather than static. In the epilogue, the Demeter of Cnidus is also linked with Rickie, who in his way is also a spiritual scion of the Greeks. As the last rays of the sun illuminate "the immortal features and the shattered knees" (308) of the goddess in Stephen's new home, we recall not only Rickie at his death when the train at the level-crossing had run over his legs but Stephen at the ford when the roseate glow from the flame boats lighted his face. The Demeter, moreover, attracts Stephen's little girl, who says goodbye to the "stone lady" as she goes out with her father to sleep on the downs. The Demeter is thus a stone figure who infuses life; paradoxically, the flesh-and-blood Agnes becomes the stony "Medusa in Arcady" who infuses death.

The relationship of the individual to Greek and Roman civilization indicates his relative worth: Rickie's bonds with Greece and Rome are intellectual, while Stephen's are physical. Upon occasion, their attitudes are almost identical; and the tragedy of their being kept apart by Mrs. Failing's manipulation of their situation becomes thereby more intense. Early in the novel Rickie responds to the poetry of the heavens whose stars the Greeks have named; Stephen's own wonder at the night is never diminished, and its stars glow brightly as he speculates on his future. With his mind, Rickie poetically elaborates his experience and places meaningful veils of gods and goddesses between himself and reality; with his body, Stephen reacts directly to outside forces, his passion for drink, for example, being met with Dionysian directness.

The boys complement each other. With the help of nature

they might indeed have been made whole in each other's presence; and Demeter, Stephen's patron goddess, would have rejoiced in the fraternal union. The very names of the horses they ride over the downs to Salisbury indicate their differing destinies as well as their native classical sympathies. Stephen, who will persist through his progeny, rides Aeneas, whose namesake had been the founder of a new kingdom. Rickie, an admirable youth deflected from his true destiny by an unfortunate love affair, rides Dido, whose namesake had met a tragic end through mistaken perceptions of her loved one's nature and purposes.

The phrase from the *Georgics* of Virgil, "O Pan, keeper of sheep," establishes Tony Failing and Rickie as mental heirs of the ancients; Stephen, as pagan in spirit. When a herd of sheep stampeded Stephen as a boy, Mr. Failing had repeated the phrase as he succored him; at school, Stephen is later punished for comically mistranslating the words, as if to demonstrate that literature itself is of subsidiary worth for one who has "been back somewhere—back to some table of the gods" (231) and has been initiated, once for all, into the company of the immortals. Rickie opens his teaching at Sawston with these Virgilian lines; their beauty is to him overwhelming, but he gets no response from the philistine boys and gives up the task of stirring them spiritually.

As a primal force and mythic presence, Stephen is compelling. Whether he is capacious enough even as an archetypal figure to absorb the forces of the intellect, man, nature, and imagination (represented by Ansell, Tony Failing, Mrs. Elliot, and Rickie) is the crux of the novel. As brute and natural man, he is persuasive, but it is doubtful that he embodies fully the classical and intellectual values. Yet Thomson's judgment that Stephen is an archetypal hero by virtue of his native force and insight, and that he supplants, as the focal center of interest, the failed hero, Rickie Elliot, is convincing.[17]

When Angus Wilson, in an interview with Forster, said he "thought most highly of *The Longest Journey* of all his novels,"[18] Forster enthusiastically endorsed this judgment. With Forster we can recognize that this novel, despite its flaws, is a work of major significance for its thematic complexity, its psychological subtlety, its human sympathy, and its suggestive artistry. *The Longest Journey* is a novel about youth, the intense idealism which kindles it, and the harrowing disillusionments which often beset it. Something of the freshness of an earlier world illuminates it; something of the elegiac sadness, inherent in the inescapable truth that beauty fades and aspirations diminish, broods over it.

Chapter Four

"Glimpses of the Diviner Wheels": *Howards End*

Division and Reconciliation:
Structure and Rhythm in *Howards End*

Howards End is the first of Forster's two main achievements, and gained for him a firm reputation when reviewers almost unanimously praised it. His memories of an idyllic boyhood spent from his fifth to his fifteenth year at Rooksnest in Hertfordshire contributed to his conception of Howards End house.[1] As early as June 26, 1908 he was thinking of a novel with contrasting cultured sisters as the chief figures, one of them marrying, with indifferent outcome, a business man.[2] The Schlegel women partly derive from Goldsworthy Lowes Dickinson's three sisters and partly from the Stephen sisters, Virginia (Woolf) and Vanessa (Bell). For the Germanic origins and relatives of the Schlegels, Forster drew upon his experience in Germany in 1905 as tutor to the children of the Countess von Arnim at Nassenheide, Pomerania. *Howards End* is, in fact, the quintessential Bloomsbury novel with its protagonist Margaret Schlegel skeptically and rationally testing social and philosophical values and balancing the polarities of the objectively real and the visionary; with its stress upon the overriding importance of personal relationships; and with its high valuation of art and culture. Margaret is also the quintessential Bloomsbury intellectual.

Although *Howards End* lacks the full control and maturity of *A Passage to India*, it is a more zestful and engaging performance. It rates highly for its incisively drawn and compelling characters; for its fusion of character and situation with idea; for the skill evinced in bringing all segments of the middle class to bear upon each other; for the interweaving of social comedy with serious, often tragic, situations; for the domestication of the romance quest in contemporary Edwardian England and the consequent interplay there of the realistic and the archetypal; and for the freshness, wit, beauty, and polish of its style.

The ramifications of the epigraph, "Only connect," are central to an understanding of *Howards End*, a novel in which the characters either make meaningful connections or else, disastrously, fail to do so. At its most explicit, the novel is concerned with the connections possible between two segments of the middle class: the Schlegels and the Wilcoxes. The Schlegel sisters are artistically inclined women of leisure, they possess humane sympathies, they espouse Forster's humanistic values, they appreciate a life-giving culture, and they recognize the graces of the spirit. Opposed to them are the practical, materialistic, enterprising, and knowledgeable Wilcoxes, who are seen as typical of the commercial class that has made England strong and wealthy: "their hands were on all the ropes." [3] As one critic has observed, the families complement each other: Henry Wilcox, the empire builder, needs "the civilizing force of liberalism"; and the Schlegels, advocates of liberalism, need Henry Wilcox's political and economic power. [4]

Ruth Wilcox is an outsider in the midst of her extroverted family; but she softens the rough edges of her husband and children and earns their respect, even if they can never understand her. Though she derives from yeoman ancestry and though she knows by instinct the details of the lives of all in her family, still she and daily life are "out of focus," as if her purposes lie elsewhere in some realm known only to her or to a few initiates. She arrives at her conclusions through intuition rather than through reason; she represents those intangible values of the spirit opposed to the material standards of her family. She embodies, moreover, the qualities associated with tradition and the earth that make for renewal.

Although she is the source of life in others, she has attained a resignation not far from indifference. She only becomes animated when she is at Howards End, her Hertfordshire house and ancestral home, or when she discusses it. Otherwise, especially in London, she reveals a fatigue and a cynicism that anticipate Mrs. Moore's nihilism in *A Passage to India*: "Mrs. Wilcox's voice, though sweet and compelling, had little range of expression. It suggested that pictures, concerts, and people are all of small and equal value" (70).

In the first pages, Ruth Wilcox at Howards End separates the incompatible Helen Schlegel and Paul Wilcox. Later, in London, she becomes the close friend of Margaret Schlegel and brings the families together. After her sudden death, the widower Henry falls in love with Margaret, possibly because she has so many of Ruth's attributes. In the course of the novel, Henry and Margaret weather some differences to become devoted husband and wife.

Considerably before Henry became romantically involved with Margaret, he had headed a family council that decided to set aside the last wish of wife and mother: to bequeath Howards End to Margaret. The fact that Ruth wished Margaret to have her most cherished possession indicates that Ruth had found in her a spiritual heir. The burning of the scrap of paper on which she signified her wish reveals how far the Wilcoxes are estranged from Ruth's values and how unreceptive they are to Margaret's similar views. But Margaret is not yet mature enough to become Ruth's successor. After tragic events partially subdue the Wilcoxes and after her relationships with Henry and Helen develop her resources to the full, Margaret is then ready to claim, by sheer spiritual authority, her inheritance. At the end, when Henry transfers the house to her and she learns for the first time about the disregarded bequest, it is fitting that she assume her symbolic role as tutelary priestess at Howards End in the succession of Ruth. During the main part of the novel, Howards End lies deserted, awaiting its rightful spiritual owner, since Ruth dies early in the action, and she alone of the Wilcox clan feels affection for the place.

The influence of Ruth Wilcox, before her death and after, brings the Schlegels and Wilcoxes to a new understanding. The influence of Leonard Bast, a clerk with intellectual pretensions whom the Schlegels first meet at a concert, divides the families. The Schlegels adopt him as protégé, and they act on Henry's advice, counseling him to change his job. He does so; but, because of fluctuations in the business world, he is ruined. Helen champions the outcast; and because she holds Henry responsible, she and the Basts storm into the opulent wedding of his daughter, Evie, at Oniton Grange in Shropshire. She demands that Henry make reparation to Leonard. The situation is complicated beyond Margaret's power to do anything for Leonard when she—and the reader—learns the full truth. Leonard's wife, Jacky, recognizes Henry as a former lover of hers in Cyprus during his marriage to Ruth. Margaret, nevertheless, decides to keep to her engagement; but in doing so, she recognizes that she can have no more to do with the Basts.

Helen, in revulsion against Henry's hostility and Margaret's indifference and in excess of pity for Leonard, gives herself to him. The result is a pregnancy which Helen conceals by deserting both lover and sister and retreating to the Continent. After Margaret's anxiety and Henry's craft lure her to Howards End, Margaret learns the reason for Helen's absence. Henry's lack of sympathy for one who has transgressed, even as he has, virtually wrecks his marriage. Because he refuses to allow her to stay with Helen for one night at Howards End and because he insists on treating Helen as fallen, Margaret decides to go to Germany with her sister to be with her during childbirth and later.

Leonard in death and Ruth Wilcox in spirit finally counter at Howards End the forces making for division between the Schlegels and the Wilcoxes. When Leonard comes to Margaret to confess his adultery with Helen, the robust and unimaginative Charles Wilcox accosts him as one who has traduced the honor of his family (Charles had learned the name of Helen's "seducer" from her brother, Tibby). Lacking vitality, strength, and assertiveness, Leonard dies after Charles beats him. Charles is convicted of manslaughter, although it is probable that Leonard died from natural causes. Henry, broken by his son's imprisonment, begs Margaret to reconsider her decision to leave him. She decides that all she can do is to bring the two people who most need her help, Henry and Helen, to Howards End to recover.

The concluding sequence, set at Howards End fourteen months after Leonard's death, has caused much discussion among Forster's critics. We must agree that, all things considered, the spectacle of a subdued Henry and a restored Helen with her healthy child, all dwelling at Howards End under Margaret's aegis, hardly represents an adequate resolution for the complex issues and relationships explored in this novel. On the realistic plane, a submissive Henry Wilcox does violence to his role in England's destiny, which Forster had intellectually fixed for him; Leonard Bast's death is fortuitous rather than inevitable; and Charles's inprisonment is arbitrary. Yet if this scene is not in all respects convincing, it is symbolically more successful than some commentators have been willing to grant.

John Edward Hardy is more positive about the conclusion than some other critics. He is persuasive when he views the final chapter as a fertility ritual over which the absent spirit of Ruth Wilcox presides and as a victory for the transcendent powers which she had embodied throughout.[5] The energies of nature with which she is identified expose both the sterile progressivism of the Wilcoxes and the abstract personalism of the Schlegels. Responsive always to spiritual modes of apprehension, however, the Schlegels quickly respond to the healing influence of house, field, tree, and vine at Howards End; for Ruth Wilcox has not educated their souls in vain. In one sense, Howards End is indeed the symbol of England, especially of the best traditions that she stands for, as Trilling maintains.[6] In another sense, Hilton Station, with its indeterminate quality suggesting both an industrial and pastoral culture, is a more precise microcosm of present-day England. Station and countryside alike are poised between these two modes of existence. Which one will survive, only the future can tell.

The triumph of Howards End and the Schlegel values is by no means assured, as London and the Wilcox values creep always closer to a house that assumes increasingly the aspect of a beleaguered fortress. The Schlegels may again at any time be called upon to defend themselves and their heritage. Far from being sentimentalized, as some think, the concluding sequence reveals a sympathetic irony. Helen's child only incidentally takes part in a realistic pastoral idyll. He is, in effect, a Blakean child, innocent perhaps but apocalyptic in his innocence, a divine child. He serves the same purpose as Gino's baby, who is killed, in *Where Angels Fear to Tread*; as the boy Stephen on the roof of Cadover house in *The Longest Journey;* as Stephen's child in that novel; and as the unborn child of Fielding and Stella in *A Passage to India*.

Ruth Wilcox continually hints at transcendent values with which all the characters must come to terms, and she becomes for George H. Thomson and others an "archetypal" character by virtue of her visionary sensitivity.[7] If we believe Margaret after her reunion with Helen, all people in the novel have their separate existences only as parts of Ruth's mind. In the last chapter Forster refers to Margaret for the first time as "Mrs. Wilcox," as if to indicate that she has now assumed Ruth Wilcox's role as mediator and peacemaker. Helen assumes Mrs. Wilcox's other role, that of mother. And Margaret has been able to come to terms with the Wilcox clan, who begin to pay her the grudging respect that Ruth Wilcox had earned before her.

Margaret's comment to Henry that "nothing has been done wrong" (342) is perhaps too sweeping; but it suggests that suffering has brought serenity, that time and tragedy have healed the divisions among the characters, and that the characters have fashioned, as a result, "the rainbow bridge" of abiding love and fulfilled connection (bringing to mind the conclusion of Wagner's *Das Rheingold* when the gods enter Valhalla over such a rainbow bridge). As in romance, the characters meet tests and survive them, except Leonard, and he is at least returned to the earth from which he sprang, before his venture into the cruel metropolis. Though the concluding sequence lacks some of the far-reaching intonations and emotional depths to be found in the greatest works that achieve mythic dimensions, still the novel as a whole often sounds such impressive, universal, cosmic overtones. Paradoxically, it gives out these reverberations all the more firmly because it so unmistakably actualizes an Edwardian culture and milieu.

As in *The Longest Journey* and *A Passage to India*, we can detect a three-part movement in this novel, even if Forster did not name the units. Like these other novels, *Howards End* moves forward in sweeping movements of related incidents and depends for unity on parallel scenes and on a repetition of incidents, themes, and symbolic images. *Howards End* thereby gains clarity of intellectual line and intricacy of design.

The theme of unity and division between the Schlegels and Wilcoxes dominates in the first section. Even the first two chapters dramatize colorfully this theme: Helen's letter to Margaret announces her engagement to Paul and then her telegram announces the break between them. The next ten chapters trace the rebuilding of the relationship between the families. This movement is brought to an end with Ruth's sudden death and her burial in Hertfordshire, the destruction of Ruth's bequest to Margaret by the members of her family who act as a "committee," and Margaret's sense of loss and her accession of wisdom as a result of her friend's passing.

For Ruth Wilcox suggests to Margaret that the spirit is immortal if the body is not, that only when one is dead does the spirit assume full authority. Margaret sees that Ruth Wilcox in death escapes "registration" and that her friend's remains are truly dust—not in the sense that she is to be soon forgotten but in the sense that she endures in so many intangible ways. The novel instructs us that, despite the existence of physical death, the force of life itself is immortal: in Hilton churchyard where Ruth lies in her grave, a laborer emblematically plucks one of Margaret's chrysanthemums for his sweetheart, and at the end of the novel the dead Leonard with the live narcissi in his hand is to be survived by a son. From Ruth Wilcox, Margaret learns that hope is certain "this side of the grave" and that "truer relationships" are possible. Later, when Margaret learns to love Howards End, she absorbs wisdom from the house and the countryside as Ruth had done before her.

The second movement of the novel stretches from Chapter 13, which picks up the Schlegels and the Basts two years after the funeral, to Chapter 30, which features Helen's interview with her brother Tibby at Oxford following the disastrous expedition with the Basts to Oniton Grange. This part of the novel develops the masterly presentation of Henry Wilcox's courtship of Margaret, her reasoned decision to marry him, and the threat to their relationship caused by the events at Oniton when Henry's past life with Jacky Bast comes to light.

In the last movement of the novel, beginning with Chapter 31, Forster analyzes Margaret's marriage, her estrangement from Helen, and then her rift with Henry. The pattern of this "movement" follows that in the second group of chapters. Again, the relationship between Margaret and Henry attains firmness and the combined influence of Helen and Leonard challenges it. Although in the preceding section Margaret had followed sexual instinct and remained loyal to Henry, she now chooses her sister as Howards End itself seems to suggest that she should; comradeship rather than sex now seems to her more important. The sanctities of long standing between herself and Helen, intensified by the presence of the Schlegel furniture in the old house, motivate her after Henry proves obdurate about Helen. Margaret's rejection of her husband is the first climax of this third section; the second is the death of Leonard, with the consequent undermining of Henry's confidence and strength. Henry's loss of nerve leads, in turn, to Margaret's muted triumph in the concluding chapter.

The presence of repeated images which attain symbolic intensity gains unity for the novel. Examples are the house at Howards End, the wych-elm tree with concealed pigs' teeth in its bark and the vine at Howards End, the Wilcox motor car, the Wilcox regimen of "telegrams and anger," the "goblin footfall" present in the Beethoven Fifth Symphony, the "abyss" close to the edge of which dwell the Basts, the grayness of London as opposed to the variegated life of the country, the hay associated with Mrs. Wilcox and later with Margaret, and the books, the bookcase, and the Schlegel sword (these latter are stored at Howards End after Margaret's marriage to Henry and unpacked by Miss Avery, Ruth Wilcox's friend and advocate). The presence of these symbols illustrates the "easy rhythm" that Forster mentions in Aspects of the Novel, as one means by which an author can unify a novel. Such a rhythm is "easy" in the sense that author and reader can with some precision isolate the elements that comprise it.

In *Howards End* Forster likewise attains a more elusive, "difficult" rhythm (also discussed in *Aspects*) in the images of flux and flow that are integral to the texture of this novel and to its deeper meaning. One of Forster's most perceptive interpreters, James McConkey, brilliantly analyzes this range of imagery.[8] He finds two contrasting kinds of movement: undirected and disintegrative movement, reflected through the meaningless activity of the city and the violent motion of the Wilcox motor car; and ordered change, reflected through the motions of nature, without which life would perish through inanition. The merging of the seasons into one another and the flow of the tides and rivers embody this regulated mobility basic to the processes of nature and their fruition.

Such "rhythms" elicit, as do similar patterns in *A Passage to India*, a sense that time stands still even as we know that it passes, that eternity lurks behind the transient shows of life, that the currents of life move inevitably to a settled calm even as they leave the chaotic present. Change and movement toward some ordered end—such is also the direction of Margaret's inner existence. But she knows that her aspirations for the eternal have, in the world of the here and now, only limited possibilities of being realized.

"A More Inward Light": Forster's Subtle Dialectic

Although the novel works in the direction of a rapprochement between the Schlegels and the Wilcoxes, a contrary movement is discernible. Critics such as Cyrus Hoy and James Hall[9] note that Margaret must not so much reconcile her standards with those of the Wilcoxes as appraise the Wilcoxes for what they are—to see critically their materialism, hypocrisy, brutality, and spiritual emptiness. The primacy of the inner life is again asserted at the novel's end, but the sisters have lost their complacency about it. "The goblin footfall," which Helen had heard in the third movement of the Beethoven Fifth Symphony, still threatens to negate a potential heroism, including Margaret's own "heroic" struggle to span the segments of the middle class; and the "abyss" on whose edge the Basts of

Edwardian England precariously live dispels an easy opti-
mism. The sisters try to alleviate squalor and injustice but
realize that their efforts may not amount to much.

Yet if Wilcox values violate much of what the Schlegels stand
for, the sisters have achieved through the Wilcoxes a new
stability. The Wilcoxes have at least preserved Howards End
from destruction and have brought the Schlegels there. Yet
what the Wilcoxes predominantly represent is "the inner darkness in high places that comes with a commercial age" (331);
and their sphere of activity is the city whose aspect, especially
in the fog, is "Satanic" and suggests "a darkening of the spirit
which fell back upon itself, to find a more grievous darkness
within" (84).

The difference between the families is that existing between
two approaches to experience. A full appreciation of the seen
or the natural, such as the Wilcoxes reveal, will lead to a steady
comprehension of life; but an informed sensitivity to the unseen or the immaterial, such as the Schlegels reveal, will lead to
a perception of life in its wholeness. Henry sees life steadily;
Margaret sees it whole. Wholeness, Forster thus implies, is
more to be valued since it will prevent the one-sidedness that
often marks the man of business and causes Margaret to break
with Henry.

The dialectic, as we have seen, brings together inner and
outer, the inner world of intellect and culture and the external
world of physical and commercial activity. Earlier critics over-
emphasized the schematic quality of the book because they
concentrated on the relationships between the Schlegels and
the Wilcoxes. More recent critics have praised the supple nature of the dialectic which is complex enough to allow for
several movements or "connections" to be made. Margaret
does connect the Wilcox prose with the Schlegel passion for life
through the understanding, sympathy, and imagination she
reveals in the relationship with Henry Wilcox; but she man-
ifests these same qualities, perhaps more spontaneously, in
establishing firmer understandings with Helen and with the
spirit of Ruth Wilcox.

Margaret is led by love to expect too much from Henry;
Helen is led by her passion for truth to anticipate too much

from her sister. From Margaret's partial success in closing the distance between the Schlegels and the Wilcoxes, Helen learns that her conception of truth had been too constricted and her championship of the Basts too impulsive. The ardor of her idealism, moreover, arouses in her a sexual emotion so absolute that it ruins Leonard more completely than Henry Wilcox could ever have done. At this point, Helen rages at Henry's having destroyed Leonard Bast twice. Blinded by the passions of the moment, she cannot judge the effects of her own actions; the result is that she ruins him a third time, despite her generous motives.

The sisters learn, Helen especially, that the credo of personal relationships is difficult to apply in the actual circumstances of life; they must learn that a belief, no matter how noble, is still a formula until the imagination makes of it a viable reality. Thus both sisters fail Leonard Bast since they regard him more as a representative of a lower social class than as a human being important in his own right. They patronize him insufferably: "Mr. Bast! I and my sister have talked you over. We wanted to help you; we also supposed you might help us" (143). "We want to show him how he may get upsides with life" (145). But Margaret's refusal to help Leonard at Oniton reveals that she values him as an individual with his own dignity; for Helen, he and his situation provide the rationale for her continuing hostility to the Wilcoxes.

Margaret learns from Helen that she has in turn been too hopeful and credulous with respect to the Wilcoxes. Anxious to give them credit for what they have done, she underestimates Henry's obtuseness and overestimates his ability to connect with people and with values opposite to his own. At the end she sees her husband realistically and no longer tries to mitigate his faults. She accepts him for what he is, without losing her affection for him. The logic of the novel may insist that Margaret and Henry have found a durable relationship; Forster's own sympathies, as James Hall points out, force us to realize that the relationship between Helen and Margaret has become the imperishable one. The sisters reassert their humanistic values and achieve a greater solidarity than do Henry and Margaret. They tacitly acknowledge a partial failure in their attempts to connect with people outside their own sphere, as with Henry Wilcox and Leonard Bast.

Still, Margaret's connection with Ruth Wilcox is possibly more important than that with Helen; for, through Ruth's example, Margaret is able to connect the intellectual world of Wickham Place and the material world of the Wilcoxes with the world of intangible and transcendent values, particularly as they find expression in Howards End house, the traditions that it represents, and the countryside that surrounds it. At the beginning Margaret is deficient in tact, understanding, and wisdom; and she comes off less well than Ruth Wilcox in the initial London encounters.

Margaret has qualities lacking in Ruth, notably a sense for social realities and an appreciation of intellect. Perhaps neither Margaret nor Ruth Wilcox is complete at their first meeting. But Ruth is more assured since her values are based upon the intuitions of the heart rather than upon the generalizations of the mind. In the course of the novel, Margaret becomes more like Ruth Wilcox, achieves much of her native insight, and acquires much of her sensitivity to the ineffable without losing her humanist's respect for reason. Through Ruth, Margaret develops a knowledge of what should be done in the crises of family life, though Ruth herself had retreated too far from the outer world to make her ideas effective in it. Yet the abrasive intellect, revealed in Margaret's London friends and sometimes in Margaret herself, is less able to cope with facts than is Ruth's instinctive wisdom.

When Margaret has grown more sensitive to the realities represented by Ruth Wilcox and has been able to remove herself from the bustle of London social life, she achieves a more dynamic reconciliation between the earthly and the transcendent than Ruth Wilcox had reached. As Ruth Wilcox had been, Margaret becomes a Demeter-figure, attaining at moments intuitions into the divine, since she, too, like Forster's version of Demeter, is not only a sibylline presence but has also transcended sex to achieve identity with a reality beyond the personal.[10] Some critics feel that Margaret loses individuality when she grows more like Ruth Wilcox, some feel that she gains in stature the nearer she approaches the ideals represented by Ruth, but all agree that there is change.[11] It is

Margaret's "profound vivacity" that distinguishes her from Ruth. Sometimes this quality leads to a commitment deeper than any shown by Ruth; sometimes, to a superficiality absent from her. On this question of Margaret's growth perhaps the judgment can stand that it is her function to develop, to illustrate the principle of "becoming," instead of remaining quiescent "at the apex of being," as Ruth Wilcox always seems to do.[12]

Margaret has to attain "proportion" by excursions toward, and withdrawals from, the extremes of experience; she can accept neither the visionary idealism of Helen without critical scrutiny nor the unmitigated pragmatism of the Wilcoxes. In the central section, as Thomson[13] points out, Helen loses her ability to connect and is unable to dominate her experience. But Margaret defines the self and its attributes with a firmer sense of reality and with a discriminating intelligence often in abeyance in both Helen and the Wilcoxes, absent in part even from Ruth Wilcox. More than Helen, certainly, Margaret "does understand herself, she has some rudimentary control over her own growth" (279).

Throughout the novel Forster prizes the values of both Margaret and Ruth Wilcox. Through Margaret, he advocates the civilized life of proportion: increased affinity with her friend's spiritual sensitivity will gradually season her rationality. Ruth's selfless, spontaneous qualities have absolute worth also; and what she stands for gains authority because Margaret intellectually values her friend's instinctive insights. Foreign to both women are the self-regarding subjectivity of Helen, the self-regarding objectivity of Paul and Charles Wilcox, the civilized artifice of Tibby Schlegel, and the unreflective worldliness of Henry Wilcox.

Margaret Schlegel ultimately does more than Ruth Wilcox to relate the strength of the spirit to mundane reality. Margaret would prevent the inner life from becoming solipsistic by projecting it outward to the everyday world, from which Ruth withdraws in tacit protest against its triviality. Margaret might also be criticizing Ruth Wilcox when she judges as inadequate Tibby's retreat from purposeful endeavor to a contemplative existence which he describes as "civilization without activity." A middle course between a withdrawn state of contemplation, represented by Ruth Wilcox, and an excessive commitment either to a social cause or to a mystical reality, represented by Helen Schlegel, is indispensable for a valid appraisal of our inner experiences. The disinterested life of the spirit must be tested, in short, by a life interested in the tangible world; and life in the material world must continually respond to the promptings of the spirit.

After World War I Forster did not relinquish entirely his earlier premise. He continued to regard the concretions of experience as important, just as important for apprehending the meaning of existence as "the unseen," the immaterial, and the sempiternal may be. He remained true, in short, to his Moorean sense of the objective reality of the phenomena that surround us. Yet Forster felt that the inner life of the spirit had become increasingly precarious in the modern age. The complications of the life within are often lost through being elusive, they are not always apparent to those who are afraid to pass beyond an outer regime of "telegrams and anger," and they are too readily discounted in a society that emphasizes secular advantages more than the affections. The mystical is not more important than an objective reality but is more likely to be overlooked.

Since the English are distrustful of the metaphysical, Ruth Wilcox fears for her material-minded progeny; and she had especially desired for Charles as a child "a more inward light." Margaret also wishes to give to her husband something more than the stolid traditions which the English ordinarily bring to one another: "this blend of Sunday church and fox-hunting" (222). Paradoxically, those individuals like Margaret and Ruth who are sensitive to the unseen most clearly see the concrete entities of their daily lives for what they are, neither ignoring them as the idealistic Helen would nor putting too much weight upon them as the materialistic Wilcoxes would.

Technique and Character Portrayal in *Howards End*

The best discussion of Forster's technique in *Howards End* is Malcolm Bradbury's.[14] He sums up what many commentators have felt: that this novel is a remarkable fusion of social realism and of poetic symbolism, its meaning at once related to men as they are and to the aspirations of those who are most gifted and perceptive. The juxtaposing of these two approaches to reality enables Forster to comment incisively upon the dualities of our experience. The interplay of the comic and the poetic animates this book as it does Forster's other novels, and perhaps Forster achieved the most subtle balancing of these two modes in *Howards End.*

As to social comedy, Forster never falters. It is the most perfectly achieved aspect of the novel, but the incisive style and the genuine beauty of many scenes haunt the memory longest. The sequences that include Aunt Julie's imbroglio with the Wilcoxes on Helen's behalf, Margaret's discussion with an uninterested Tibby about his future, the Wilxoxes' committee-like manner and actions concerning Ruth's bequest, the exaggerated protectiveness of Henry Wilcox and his friends for the women whom they bring down from London to Shropshire for Evie's wedding, the good-natured ineptitude of Dolly Wilcox whenever she confronts Henry or her husband Charles, the first steps in the courtship between Margaret and Henry at Simpson's Restaurant in London, and the distraught Helen Schlegel's conference with a placid Tibby in his Oxford rooms after the Oniton affair—all reveal Forster's expertise in the comic mode. Comedy modulates into sardonic satire when Charles voices his contempt for the "artistic beastliness" of the Schlegels, when he feels at Oniton Grange that Margaret might be about to tempt him sexually, when Margaret's sophisticated friends fail to understand Ruth Wilcox at the London luncheon, and when Aunt Julie and her German relative Frieda Mosebach chauvinistically extol the merits of their separate countries.

Although Forster reveals his standards directly or by implication through all his characters, Margaret Schlegel is his chief assimilative and questing intelligence. At times, as she matures, she achieves those wider perspectives and depths of insight that betoken vision, and they endow her with the qualities of the seeker for illumination characteristic of the protagonists of romance. She is also the ardent advocate of

Forster's humanistic values with her emphasis on individuality, self-fulfillment, personal relationships, imaginative
sensitivity, sympathy and compassion, knowledge and understanding, and a vital culture.

For most readers Margaret is a sympathetic character. At
points, she is a bit too assured of her values (the Wilcoxes were
"deficient where she excelled," 103) or too complacent about
her own existence ("culture had worked in her own case,"
115); she may strike us as a bit overbearing toward the Wilcoxes. Forster is so closely identified with her, both as protagonist and as spokesman, that the distance between himself
and her is too narrow for her always to be dramatically effective in enunciating ideas. Still, his humanistic gospel is attractive enough so that she is not reduced appreciably as a character
when she engages in abstract discourse. For the most part, too,
she embodies Forster's views instead of merely stating them.
She believes in being true to her own standards and in applying
them, with varying degrees of success, to the people and the
crises she encounters in her somewhat refractory existence.

Ruth Wilcox acts as a brooding presence and pervades the
novel the more completely by virtue of her death early in the
action. At times she does suggest the "greatness" that Forster
imputes to her. She is believable as a natural aristocrat and as
one who illustrates "the deeply moral quality of taste, which
the intellect is powerless by itself to attain." [15] Perhaps because
she is so real as a crotchety woman, she fails to persuade fully
on a more philosophical plane. As a presiding genius and
guardian figure, she does not quite overspread the novel. She
is, in fact, sometimes static and two-dimensional in contrast
with Mrs. Moore, the more fully envisioned guardian presence
in *A Passage to India*.

Forster is successful with Helen Schlegel, a girl who somewhat stridently seeks those spiritual heights where Ruth Wilcox dwells serenely by instinct. She disregards, moreover, the
truth that the immaterial must reveal itself through the material. She learns at Howards End late in the novel the reality and
consecrating power of the actual; previously, she had been the
"idealist" whose intuitions are disconnected with the facts that
should provide them with a strong and solid base. In any case,

she finds in her reunion with Margaret that the house, the tree, and the furniture give her a surer basis for a renewed relationship than intellectual discussion does. Helen, who broods on the unseen, lacks the control that mystical experience often confers; rather, she is motivated by instinct and passion; and, for a lover of the absolute, she is highly sexed. Though she is critical of those who fail in their responsibilities, she is appalled by the responsibilities that originate in her own yielding to passion. As for Leonard, Helen finds that cash payment is easier than sustaining a difficult relationship.

The affair with Leonard has often been considered unreal,[16] and something may be said for the view that Helen as an Edwardian lady would not have given herself to him. Such a view minimizes the element of passion in Helen, her great resentment against the Wilcoxes, and the "tense, wounding excitement" suffusing her conduct at Oniton. Forster was also demonstrating in Helen's lapse that bodily passion is often a concomitant of strong intellectual commitment. Her charm, cordiality, and generosity are genuine; and her defects are the easily forgiven ones that derive from excessive feeling, from the warm subjectivity of the romantic temperament. Even while she is pregnant with an illegitimate child, she suggests the seraphic quality of a madonna as the vine at Howards End frames her head and shoulders while the sun "glorifies" her hair.

Some central insights in the novel are Helen's. She responds the most spontaneously to Beethoven's Fifth Symphony and thereby dramatizes some of Forster's central values. She hears in the music the eternal conflict between human aspiration and the "goblin footfall" of evil which challenges heroism but also provides it with its excuse for being. Forster, like Beethoven and Helen, hears the goblin footfalls in the distance and knows that any triumph can only be muted and short-lived. Helen's values and insights, in short, have intrinsic worth, even if some of them are distorted and only partly true. She is a complicated and fascinating character.

In a well-known interview Forster asserted that he brought off the home life of Leonard and Jacky Bast, though he knew nothing at first hand about it.[17] He did know something about individuals from the lower fringe of the middle class, however, as a result of his experiences of teaching at the Working Men's College. Though Forster's critics have often viewed the characterization of Leonard adversely, Frederick J. Hoffman's view of him as a "most remarkable portrait, a mixture of hero and caricature" is an informed judgment.[18] In any event, Forster admirably projects into the sequences including Leonard and Jacky the elements of tenderness, squalor, humor, and vulgarity.

Leonard in action is a vital and interesting individual, though Forster deflates him unnecessarily at times by belittling comment. Actually, Leonard has, as Cyrus Hoy maintains,[19] the qualities in latent form that make Margaret heroic—"honor, courage, strength." Implied is a link between the two when they both cut fingers on framed portraits. Leonard is linked also to Helen by virtue of the Cupid figurines on his lodging mantlepiece; we recall Helen's musing on the Cupids in the fretted ceiling of the concert hall and deciding she could never marry a man like them. In a moment of vehemence, we can infer, she later gives herself to a man whom she could never bring herself to marry.

Indeed, Forster's treatment of Leonard is at once deft and heavy-handed. At the close of the novel, Leonard is beaten by Charles with the flat of Ernst Schlegel's sword in a parody of the knighthood ceremony. This parodic use of a heroic ritual emphasizes the nonheroic qualities of Charles and the pitiful presence as well as the submerged potential of Leonard. Leonard's death, as it derives from the toppled Schlegel bookcase, is contrived, however, making him too openly a physical victim of the culture that he had sought. Elsewhere in the novel, Leonard is more convincingly a victim of pressures beyond his power to control. At Oniton, for example, his shabbiness contrasts with the opulence of Evie's wedding; this scene suggests that the impersonal forces by which the Wilcoxes prosper have operated at the expense of Leonard and his class.

As for Henry Wilcox, critics generally agree that he is one of Forster's best creations. There is little question of Henry's reality, and Forster analyzes acutely his motives and personality. Forster conveys well his sexual charm, his forthright energy, and his commanding presence, depicting him as a feudal lord of sorts who demands admiration from his family and the women he "protects." Forster establishes his insensitivity, his distrust of emotion, his evasiveness and lack of candor, his deficiency in generosity and in imagination, his complacency, and his inability to take criticism. On the whole, a negative impression emerges and a convincing one. This negative valuation, however, goes counter to the achievements, physical and moral, that Forster imputes to the Wilcoxes as empire-builders and developers of wealth. A major flaw is Forster's failure to illustrate the Wilcox virtues in sequences as symbolically arresting as those in which he exemplifies the Wilcox defects.

Critics such as F. R. Leavis and J. K. Johnstone have considered Margaret's marriage to Henry as improbable or reprehensible.[20] Yet Henry's animal magnetism and his energies are never in question; and they provide a firm basis for Margaret's yielding to him. It is natural enough that opposites like Henry and Margaret should attract each other and have a union which is happy on the surface but that their opposed values should sometimes clash and disturb the harmony of their relationship. The critics who have emphasized the "unreality" of the marriage have not fully appreciated, perhaps, the strains inherent in relationships involving temperamental opposites. The presentation of Henry's and Margaret's life together is vulnerable, however, to the extent that Forster allows his own antipathy to Henry to outrun his intellectual valuation of Henry's type—in contrast to previous judgments, to describe him, for example, through Margaret after the fiasco over Helen, as "rotten at the core."

The characters in *Howards End* are arresting, the ideas conveyed are stimulating, and the organization is subtle. Yet the most lasting impression derives from Forster's brilliant style, which at its best attains an incandescent realization of the actual, or an intensity associated with visionary experience. Light, color, and sound form the fabric of a prose that suggests more than it states and that opens out to the transcendent through the illuminated perceptions of the present moment. The poetry is authentic in such sequences as Margaret's

listening to the motions of the tidal waters on the Thames
embankment, the colorful Maytime garden at Howards End
on Margaret's first visit, the mist-enshrouded landscape and
the ceaseless murmuring of the river at Oniton Grange, Margaret's walk at Hilton on her second visit to Howards End
through the chestnut avenue to the old church, and the en-
chanted moonlight night at the house when the sisters achieve
their deepest accord. Such scenes do suggest that Margaret's
"belief in the eternity of beauty" is no idle or sentimental
formulation; and they convey to us, if fleetingly, "glimpses of
the diviner wheels" (330), suggestions of the "ultimate harmony" we may be moving toward, and some notion that
certain sense experiences are at times "apparelled in celestial
light,/ The glory and the freshness of a dream."

Chapter Five
"Eternal Differences Planted by God": *Maurice* and the Later Tales

"Dedicated to a Happier Year": *Maurice*

After writing four outstanding novels, Forster came to feel that he had exhausted the possibilities of writing fiction on socially acceptable subjects, as he complained in a diary entry for June 16, 1911: "Having sat for an hour in vain trying to write a play, will analyse causes of my sterility. . . . Weariness of the only subject that I both can and may treat—the love of men for women & vice versa." [1]

Perhaps frustration of this kind prevented the completion of *Arctic Summer*, the novel upon which Forster embarked in 1910. The main version remains impressive in the parts (the first five chapters) that Forster revised for a reading at the Aldeburgh Festival on June 10, 1951. The first four of these chapters form a unit, almost as if they were a completed short story, and are forceful as they expose the disastrous effects that an unimaginative woman, Venetia Borlase, has upon the dynamic, potentially heroic Lieutenant March and the relationship that had begun to flourish between him and her husband, Martin Whitby, the type of the civilized intellectual. On the platform at Basle, March had saved Martin from falling under a train, and a friendship rapidly developed between them. Venetia destroys March's desire to visit Tramonta Castle by telling him how overpowered her husband had been there in recognizing a striking likeness between March and one of his ancestors, depicted in a fresco as a soldier fighting the Turks at

Lepanto in the sixteenth century. In effect, she invades his privacy and attempts to discuss, in an intolerable way, matters that he holds sacrosanct. Although these chapters are compelling, Forster proved unequal to developing further the relationship between the men and abandoned the novel in 1912.

But a visit to Edward Carpenter and George Merrill freed his creative energies and inspired him to write his homosexual novel, *Maurice*, which he finished quickly in 1914.[2] Forster revised it at various times after 1924, particularly the last chapters; and it was posthumously published in 1971. His stories on homosexual themes, also appearing after his death and dating from 1922 and after, demonstrate that he continued to write fiction after *A Passage to India* (1924), though he did not publish any more. Because these stories and *Maurice* are thematically related and come in large part from his later life (*Maurice* was extensively revised as late as 1959–60) we can view them together. In these writings, Forster, in essence, defends the "eternal differences, planted by God in a single family" (338), so eloquently described by Margaret Schlegel in the conclusion to *Howards End*, even when, as in the chief characters of these writings, the differences may involve socially proscribed forms of sexuality.

The plot and situation in *Maurice* are relatively simple. Maurice Hall comes out of prosperous, smug, bourgeois England before the Great War, and he in some sense represents the values that Forster in his earlier novels had associated with Sawston. Maurice is also the opposite of what Forster considered himself to be, since Maurice is "someone handsome, healthy, bodily attractive, mentally torpid, not a bad businessman and rather a snob."[3] He is "normal" except for his emotional, and especially his sexual, temperament. If it were not for this disturbing, unaccountable, and bizarre element in his nature, he would undoubtedly have accepted his bourgeois heritage. But the full acceptance of his sexual disposition at the end of the novel will make him permanently a rebel. The choice for him is final, when he and his lower-class lover, Alec Scudder, spend the night together in London, an act which entails Maurice's foregoing of a dinner party, of consequence to him as a member of a brokerage firm.

The transcendent values of the earlier novels become concentrated in the sexual life in *Maurice*. Because Forster made specific what had been ineffable in the early novels, *Maurice* loses a degree of resonance. The characters are less complex, and there is less accommodation, too, to the conventions of romance. *Maurice* is, for the first three-fourths of it, mainly a realistic novel in which Forster depicts the trials experienced by the protagonist, Maurice Hall, as he matures into a wavering, and then a certain, knowledge of his own nature: that he is homosexual and that he cannot change to conform to the behests of Edwardian society. The awareness that he achieves is more specialized than that attained by the other protagonists in Forster's novels; it is less metaphysical in nature and less ineffable. The book is thinner than Forster's other novels because there is less tension between the real and the transcendent, and an expansive symbolism is in abeyance. But the book is by no means negligible, and its merit becomes more firm the more one studies it.

Except for an increasingly obtrusive sense of his homosexuality, Maurice's experiences as a boy and young man are typical of those of his class. He attends preparatory school until adolescence, when one of the masters tries to communicate to him knowledge about sex. But Mr. Ducie's embarrassment and tactlessness not only confuse Maurice but arouse in him disgust for the man's furtiveness. Public school at Sunnington brings no significant developments, other than Maurice's being attracted to a number of his classmates. At Cambridge Maurice has his first significant erotic encounter, with Clive Durham, an intellectual and scion of a landed family whose estate is Penge on the border between Somerset and Wiltshire and whose circumstances and influence are declining. At the university Clive finds illumination in the writings of Plato and a recognition of the truth about himself: he is attracted sexually to men. Clive would agree with Plato's characteristic view, that such love should be kept pure and spiritually intense by refraining from a consummation of passion.

Maurice at first rejects in horror Clive's advances; but after a period of introspection and a reading of the *Symposium*,

Maurice realizes that he, too, is constituted as Clive and that he is drawn sexually to men. He discovers, in fact, that the idealism and the brutality he had known separately all his life now fuse into love. From this point Maurice is more advanced than Clive, who discounts the brutal or the physical; the denial of this element in their relationship increasingly frustrates Maurice and contributes in a subterranean way to its disintegration. Clive at first rejects Maurice's expressions of contrition. A reconciliation follows when, acting on instinct, Maurice enters Clive's room by the window and, as he does so, hears his sleeping friend call out, "Maurice." Maurice and Clive continue as "platonic" friends for some years after Cambridge, until a period of illness and of subsequent travel in Greece brings Clive to a realization of the fact that he is now interested in women and has become "normal," even, as he says, "against my will."

When Clive rejects him as intimate, Maurice feels that a calamity has overtaken him; only a determined effort of will keeps him functioning when all magic and purpose seem to have gone from life. The rest of the novel, in fact, centers on Maurice's adjustments to his changed relationship with Clive, and, with compassion and insight, on his alien existence in a hostile world that does not understand or even tolerate the homosexual temperament. Clive feels physical revulsion toward Maurice and marries a colorless woman from his own class, Anne Woods. Passion, though not tenderness, is lacking in this relationship, passion having receded from Clive's temperament with his rejection of Maurice. The physical demands of Maurice's being and also a contrary desire to establish, if at all possible, a heterosexual basis for his existence increasingly trouble him. He enlists the services of Dr. Barry, the family doctor, who solves Maurice's problem by contemptuously dismissing it; and Maurice also seeks the services of a hypnotist, a Mr. Lasker-Jones, in the attempt to exorcise an alienating, socially reprehensible element from his nature.

A fatality beyond his power to modify soon overtakes Maurice. On a visit to Clive and his wife, Clive offends him by a lack of cordiality, and he is attracted, almost in spite of himself, to a personable, apparently bisexual gamekeeper on

Clive's estate, Alec Scudder. In a scene recalling the appearance to Clive of Maurice as a saving god who mysteriously comes out of nowhere to help one who is distraught, Alec correspondingly ministers to Maurice's need for completeness at a time of stress, climbing a ladder and coming through a window at Maurice's cry of "Come." In joining forces in a cricket match the next day, they pitch their youth and vitality against the physical desuetude of Penge estate and the desiccated Durhams.

The relationship between Maurice and Alec is an uneasy one, and Forster traces its implications fully, truthfully, and compassionately. The two communicate and understand completely with their bodies, though differences in social class and cultural background at first divide them. With their conscious selves the men act as social convention would dictate, Maurice as snob and Alec as blackmailer. Maurice must overcome his sense of shame at intimacy with one from Alec's class, while Alec must overcome his social resentments. Finally, the impulses of the heart and "the holiness of the heart's imagination" triumph over prescriptive mores. When the men are strangers, love is still in part for them "panic in essence" (226), the very intensity of ecstasy begetting feelings of uncertainty and fear as the surges of emotion dissipate. When Alec does not show up to embark for Argentina to which he planned to emigrate, Maurice divines that Alec has remained in England on his account. Maurice rushes to the boathouse at Penge to find an eager and tender Alec. Their projected life as lovers implies a continuing exile from middle-class England. So Maurice has passed from conformist to permanent rebel, and he deems that the bourgeois world of England is indeed well lost for love of Alec.

The chief limitation of the novel inheres in Forster's conception of his protagonist. In order for Maurice to illustrate the difficulties that an average man would face if he were to express homosexual urges, Forster drastically limited him as a human being and downplayed him. Maurice seldom expanded, then, to the point that he threatened Forster's austere control of him; Forster was in little danger of Maurice's "running away" with him as his best conceived characters often did.

The apathy and philistinism, so often characteristic of Maurice, generate little positive effect. One does not identify readily with a man for whom Italy is "well enough in spite of the food and the frescoes" and for whom Greece "sounds out of repair" (111). Forster wished to be objective in portraying Maurice, but in distancing and diminishing him, he endangered compelling literary treatment of an unusual social question. An average man in society is not necessarily a typical presence in a literary work, and this discrepancy may not have been quite apparent to Forster. Maurice's intellectual incapacity is negative, rather than positive in its impact. Forster intended that Maurice should connect all the fragments about him, as Margaret Schlegel had tried to do in *Howards End*,[4] but Maurice is not conspicuously adept in doing so or especially convincing when he tries to work outward from his particular situation to a defining of larger issues. Forster is at the same time excessively critical of Maurice's spiritual nature and intellectual equipment and then indulgent toward him in relating his adventures and disappointments in love. Granted, acuteness of insight is shown in the charting of Maurice's perplexities and frustrations, but an obsessive interest in them also makes Forster at times overemphatic in presenting his protagonist.

Forster's touch becomes firmer as the novel progresses and Maurice emerges, on account of his valid sufferings, as an individual of stature. In the last half of the novel Forster closes the distance between himself and his protagonist and depicts his perplexities and difficult choices with complete sympathy. Only when Maurice has lost in Clive's love everything making life worthwhile, only when absolute loneliness overpowers him, only when but for a sense that love does somewhere exist he would have ended his life ("a lamp that would have blown out, were materialism true," 143) does he achieve authentic dignity and true self-awareness. Much poignancy and justified despair develop when, after the affair with Clive, Maurice seeks help from Dr. Barry, Mr. Lasker-Jones, and others and finds only silence and evasion: "On all other subjects he could command advice, but on this, which touched him daily, civilization was silent" (156).

The strength of *Maurice* lies in Forster's presentation of Maurice's principal relationships with other men and in its satiric treatment of middle-class and aristocratic values.

Clive Durham is interesting as the type of man who, in literature as in life, sublimates homosexual love, as Goldsworthy Lowes Dickinson had done, and also many of the Cambridge Apostles who later formed Bloomsbury, including—for many years—Forster himself. For Clive, therefore, love tended to remain a mental concept and abstraction; and it is significant that he regards Pallas Athena rather than Eros or Dionysus as his patron deity when he visits Greece. Clive's idealized conceptions may partly motivate his later abandonment of homosexuality: one set of ideas yields to another the more readily if the concrete and personal are in abeyance. In Clive the change from an idealized homosexuality to a heterosexual sensualism is somewhat improbable, if it may be psychically still possible. In any case, the change is too entire for the greatest number of elements of conflict to be effectively present. For the most part, Forster articulates well the heightened comradeship between Clive and Maurice, maintained over several years; and the relationship is genuine and moving, revealing affection without sentimentality. As a result, it ought to have been as absorbing in its termination as it was in its inception and growth. The rift between them is too sudden, Clive being presented thereafter as a denier of life rather than as one who chooses another kind of life. Clive's revulsion from Maurice dominates the breach between the two rather than regret that love for Maurice must yield to another kind of love, desirable in a different way.

As for the relationship between Maurice and Alec, Forster establishes its beginnings, development, and fruition persuasively, inevitably, and authoritatively. In the beginning Alec is but a presence felt in the background. His refusal of a five shilling tip, his helping to move a piano and his lingering behind to obtrude on Maurice as the latter selects a book, his half-hearted apology for refusing the tip, his attempts to force his presence on Maurice by sending him messages after dinner, his firm but fleeting embrace of Maurice in the darkened wood, his captaining of a cricket team on which Maurice serves, and his peering into Maurice's carriage through a hedge of dog-roses beside the road are all incidents that embody a subterranean shock of recognition between the two men and set up a tension in Maurice between a full confronting of his situation and a desire to evade it. Maurice must learn not to sin against the light; he must choose fulfillment in passion rather than comfort in convention, the same but somewhat easier choice that Lucy Honeychurch must make in *A Room with a View*.

Alec Scudder is ambiguous enough as a force to cause Maurice discomfort: whether he is to be comrade or devil, Maurice cannot quite predict. The connection between them does, indeed, demand this ambiguity. The presence of this psychic split in Alec argues, moreover, that Maurice's continued life with him could hardly have been harmonious. What is false in their relationship is the stated happy outcome and the direct rendition of passion, not the encounter itself and its equivocal aspects. For good or ill, Alec is Maurice's "double," the "friend" for whom he has always searched but a demon lover also, a passionate rather than a kind man. Alec's blackmail attempts hint, too, at sadism and a desire for mastery. The sequence in the British Museum where the two men are locked in conflict on the surface while their deeper natures reverberate with ever-increasing accord is absorbing. The sequence is authentic, too, to the degree that fear and cruelty are present always—or nearly so—in the souls of those who love, the fear perhaps engendering the cruelty. Because of all the obstructions in their way, there is sadness as well as triumph in their night together in London, to which Maurice accedes "in affectionate yet dejected tones" (227).

The scenes between the two are authentic so long as Forster concentrates on their external facets or analyzes in them some conflict or general activity. What is not so convincing is his direct description of ecstasy between the two, or the intimate conversations between them. Forster does not excel in depicting passion directly: his vocabulary is flat, trite, or lush: " 'You all, right, Maurice? . . . . You comfortable? Rest your head on me more, the way you like more . . . that's it more, and Don't You Worry. You're With Me. Don't Worry' " (228).

Much more successful is Forster's use of nature in the concluding episodes. Through its means, he does hint with authority at the emotional transports to be enjoyed by the reunited lovers. In the night they are free to receive the blessing of nature: when they leave the British Museum, they exchange with relief and enthusiasm the heated building and "the sordid day" for the rain and darkness. Forster's imaging of the brilliant sunset sky as the backdrop to Maurice's happiness on his way back to Alec is far more compelling than anything the lovers will say or have said. The nocturnal scents from the apricot tree and the evening primrose flowers at Penge also anticipate quite credibly the intensity of consummated love. These flowers are emblematic of the fulfilled psyche and have that connotation even for Clive as he sees the Hall sisters expand in their presence when Maurice, who inhibits the sisters, is absent. Primarily, however, the primroses and their fragrance are associated with Maurice's homosexual fulfillment with Alec. A mound of their incandescent petals remains at the close of the novel to remind Clive of the Maurice who has just left him forever.

If *Maurice* partly fails because direct summary exceeds a dramatization of issues, many truly Forsterian scenes do occur; for example, the great scene at the British Museum. Likewise memorable is the day of pagan rout after Clive and Maurice are reconciled at Cambridge, and they go into the country in Maurice's sidecar. There is the tense time when Clive breaks with Maurice, and Maurice attacks him, only to be deflected when Clive lets fall the key to the room to which Ada Hall, Maurice's sister, had just retreated. The scene wherein Maurice unfairly lashes out at Ada because he is jealous of her interest in the reoriented Clive (and Clive's in her) reveals the cruelty that is the underside of passion. In a sequel when she becomes engaged to another Maurice tries to apologize, but Forster notes that the harm has been done: ". . . he had insulted her centrally, and marred the dawning of a love" (142). The scenes with Mr. Lasker-Jones, the hypnotist, are also excellent: Maurice is within an ace of being "reclaimed," but Alec comes to his mind and determines absolutely the course of Maurice's life.

As in the other prewar novels Forster satirizes middle-class

values, implicitly when Maurice at first unthinkingly embraces
them and explicitly when, in moments of perception, he criticizes his compeers for specific defects. The even, unexciting
life of suburbia almost claims him, "a land of facilities, where
nothing had to be striven for, and success was indistinguish-
able form failure" (16). At Cambridge, under the influence of
awakening love for Clive, he gains some insight into the desiccation of his own class, especially its so-called religion. The
Hall family can only understand religion as it relates to their
status in the community; it is a matter of forms for them,
Maurice thinks, and only comes alive when critics challenge it.
The pain that derives from opposition to their set values consti-
tutes religious emotion for his people; their commitment,
Maurice thinks, is not to the Bible, the Prayer Book, the
Sacraments, Christian ethics, or anything spiritual. At Easter
no one notices that he does not "communicate." This apathy
and hypocrisy bother him far more than forthright opposition
to his irreligion would have: "Did society, while professing to
be so normal and sensitive, really mind anything?" (53) he
wants to know. An instance of the petty propriety that motivates his family occurs in Ada Hall's distress at having a nurse
in the house: "Nurses are not nice. No nice girl would be a
nurse. If they are you may be sure they do not come from nice
homes, or they would stop at home" (108).

Maurice is the only one of Forster's novels that satirizes the
nineteenth-century landed gentry, in the tradition of Carlyle's
Past and Present, Chekhov's *The Cherry Orchard*, and Shaw's
Heartbreak House. The satire represents Forster at his best;
and the scenes at Penge are excellent and characteristic. In
decline Clive's family connotes the decadence of an aristocracy
which, along with the materialism of the middle class, has
loosened the fabric of English life. Penge is a symbol of a failing
England ". . . both house and estate were marked, not indeed
with decay, but with the immobility that precedes it" (86). The
leaking roof is emblematic of the inefficiency of this class, its
internal decay, its fecklessness, and its lack of will. The rain, as
it comes in unchecked from the outside, may also symbolize
the intrusion of nature, a life-giving element, an unwelcome
reality into cloistered lives. Maurice comes to feel that Clive's

class is no longer fit to exert power, "to set standards or control the future" (239); and Clive himself, Maurice thinks, has deteriorated from the open, honest, forthright, idealistic pagan prince he once had known. The disintegration of his class parallels this personal decline and may have contributed to it. With Clive, in the years since Cambridge, respectability rather than life has triumphed; the result is Clive's "thin, sour disapproval, his dogmatism, the stupidity of his heart" (244), when Maurice tells him of his love for Alec. For the earlier and more critical Clive, his class combines material values with lack of imagination, ". . . worldliness . . . with complete ignorance of the World" (96).

When compared to Forster's other novels *Maurice* is a slighter performance. Yet it is better than most critics have conceded. It has much to fascinate and to delight, and its full flavor comes through only after one has become accustomed to Forster's unusual subject, his directness of narrative line, and his suspension of irony toward his protagonist. The lack of complication in *Maurice*, its constricted scope, and its limited perspective detract from its stature. But Forster's detached manner, his sustained compassion, his sporadic displays of insight, and his stylistic power all assert that *Maurice* is his novel.

Tales of Passion: The Later Short Stories

The later stories in *The Life to Come*, all of them dating from 1922 and after, dramatize homosexual themes. Consequently, Forster felt that he could not publish them for fear of incurring censorship or notoriety or both. If they had been known before his death, they would have modified the then-current image of Forster as the saintly sage of King's College, a view propounded especially by his Indian admirers.[5] The stories are in large part sexual wish fulfillment, too often presented in a moral and spiritual vacuum, too often only tenuously referred to the circumstances of social life except in "Arthur Snatchfold," "Dr. Woolacott," "The Life to Come," and "The Other Boat." Sensuality allied to violence, an Olympian view that sex is its own excuse for being, and a Dionysian presump-

tion that passional excess is a desirable norm scarcely comport
with the image of equability and infallible wisdom that the
public then held of Forster and that he apparently encouraged
it to hold.

Some of these late tales do not have much substance. "What
Does It Matter? A Morality" is an inconclusively dramatized
fable; the unrealized intention is more compelling than Forster's skill in executing it. Still, a refreshing point is made: the
sexual lives of public officials are no one else's business, a
principle which the Henry Wilcoxes or the Charles Wilcoxes
or the Herbert Pembrokes of this world would never care to
acknowledge, and a principle which the Anglo-Indians of *A
Passage to India* also repudiate in their wolf-pack persecution
of Aziz and his defender, Fielding. Under an enlightened
dictator, the Pottibakians learn the wisdom of his program,
"Do as you wish." "The Classical Annex" is a *jeu d'esprit*, in
which a staid museum curator, fearful of pagan responsive-
ness, sexuality, and amorality, wishes to exorcize them. Without thinking of the consequences, he makes the sign of the
cross when an amorous male statue comes alive and frolics with
his son. The result of the curator's gesture is a celebrated
statuary group of wrestlers and a lost son: the cross can arrest
life but there is no comparable gesture by which arrested life
can later be restored once it has been taken away. So much for
Christianity and its repressive asceticism.

"The Obelisk" is a more interesting and firmly realized tale
than most critics have granted. An unlikely middle-class husband and wife have unexpected encounters, each with a sailor,
at a seaside resort that is celebrated for an obelisk on the top of
a nearby hill. On the way to view it, husband and wife each
make a detour to engage in a brief sexual venture. Neither one
ever reaches the obelisk; or if the obelisk is a phallic symbol,
each one does reach it figuratively. The wife finds out by
chance that her husband has lied to her in saying he got to see
the obelisk, and she notes a smugness in her husband that she
can now attribute to an experience similar to hers. The tale is
unusual in being presented from the woman's point of view; it
is her sexual experience that is recreated in detail, with sympathy and intensity. The tale reveals, perhaps, that the hetero-

sexual element in personal relationships was a reality for Forster as a social commentator, even if it was not the reality that he preferred.

"The Torque" is a somewhat simplistic tale in the contrast that it offers between Perpetua, the soured ascetic Christian who devotes her life to the glorification of God, and her brother Marcian, an easy-going, sensuous, life-loving pagan who does not mind saving his sister from sexual "dishonor" even if it involves his own rape by the barbarian, Euric. The removed setting in history of this anti-Christian parable provides Forster less with a viable distancing of his materials than with a means whereby he can escape the fullest ramifications of the conflict between sex and Christianity. Forster is indulgent in presenting homosexuality and quite casual in caricaturing Christian renunciation. He cannot admit that, in some lights, the sincerity of a person like Perpetua might be creditable. As a repressive force, she is exorcized by her death in the basilica that she insists on entering in order to quell the supposedly evil spirits in its luminous depths; these spirits seem to be concentrated there in the now glowing golden torque that Euric had given Marcian. Whether Marcian continues to love men is not clear. He apparently was the incestuous lover of his adoring young sisters and becomes the center of a prosperous existence on the family farm. As a man ever more deeply in rapport with the earth, he flourishes as the Christian influence of his sister wanes.

In "Arthur Snatchfold," a more considerable tale, the homosexuality is again explicit, but a sense of complication results when it is pitted against the law. Sir Richard Conway's gratification of passion with Arthur Snatchfold, a milkman, is a casual and yet satisfying and vitalizing experience for the older man. Forster also establishes, with some authority, the impasse which then results when the law—as the embodiment of inflexible convention—proscribes a genuine human impulse. Snatchfold, a primitive man with a highly developed ethical sense, refuses to implicate his lover. Conway emerges as a hypocrite with a conscience, and Snatchfold, because of his loyalty to a slight acquaintance, emerges as a martyr to communal outrage. Conway is unequal in moral courage to his humble lover, but his remorse is intense if ineffectual; the impasse calls for a greatness of which he is incapable. As Forster presents the situation, neither Snatchfold nor Conway can be regarded as criminals; their only sin has been the gratifying of a basic impulse that was affectionate as well as self-serving. There is neither affection nor life present in the banal middle-class culture with its pursuit of industrial wealth and social prestige, which Forster satirizes in the first pages of the story.

"Dr. Woolacott" is concerned, as in part were many of Forster's earlier stories, with the shifting boundaries between the actual and the supernatural. A pleasant youth, who jumps over Clesant's wall, represents vitality and, incidentally, homosexual passion. His presence is associated with the music of the violin which the retainers in the house hear, the music which Dr. Woolacott had forbidden Clesant to play: it is a disruptive force symbolic to Clesant of an unutterable yearning. The boy is at once a war veteran, a farmhand, and a supernatural presence—a Stephen Wonham whose natural force is purer and more disembodied. Despite his alleged curative powers, Dr. Woolacott represents, in contrast, the force of death as he practiced his profession in the trenches of World War I and as he now assumes dominance over passive men like Clesant. The boy and Woolacott struggle for the soul of Clesant who is tempted to follow the regime that Woolacott has prescribed for him, in order to live to the year 2000. In the concluding sequence Clesant embraces the farmboy who once again appears, this time as a tangible spirit force. Clesant no longer hesitates to risk death, now that he knows that a more intense kind of inner wholeness will develop from his relationship with the boy. Clesant's death ensues—a transfiguration rather than an annihilation, since it is the quality of life, not the mere continuation of it, that is a primary value.

"The Life to Come" develops the same contrast as "The Torque" between the sensual and the ascetic, the worldly and the otherworldly, the flesh and the spirit, the so-called perversions of the flesh and the real deterioration of the spirit resulting from a denial of the senses. In exploring so consistently these dichotomies this work is the nearest in spirit to *Howards*

End among these posthumously printed stories. Initially, the Christian Pinmay is more sympathetic than Perpetua in "The Torque," possibly because he goes counter to official Christian views on sex; and his struggles and conflicts persist. He becomes contemptible only when he gives over conflict, denies his own sexual nature, and adopts conventional attitudes. Whether he could have resolved his problem in any way that could countenance homosexual passion is doubtful; but if the relationship with Vithobai, his native lover, meant all that it should have to him, Pinmay might at least have resigned from the church and left the African scene.

Pinmay is caught between a religion that forbids the gratifying of homosexual desire and his instinctive drive to satisfy such passion; he feels strong love but a stronger guilt, and he also lacks the decisiveness to end a relationship by honestly appraising it for what it is. As a Christian missionary, he extinguishes unsanctified desire (he cannot do otherwise), though he becomes unchristian in spirit by so doing, reverting to a repressive and vindictive Old Testament morality. So Forster implies that the suppression of any potentially fulfilling natural impulse can result in spiritual disaster. The two men become inhuman as a result of the denial of the passion that had once existed between them. As death from consumption impends, Vithobai reasserts his kingly prerogatives and stabs Pinmay so that his former lover will reach "the life to come" before he does. Vithobai now assumes the temporal supremacy that Christianity, in his later life, had denied to him. In this parable Forster emphasizes simply that love is love even when it is homosexual. He also maintains that a codified morality, an institutionalized religion, and a monolithic industrialism can all become dehumanizing forces.

In "The Other Boat" Forster skillfully demonstrated the unforeseen consequences of uncontrolled passion when that passion can only be surreptitiously gratified. Through their relationship, a British captain, Lionel March, and an Indian merchant, Cocoanut, conjoin precipitately two races, two notions of sexuality, two moralities, two modes of life, and two civilizations. In an enlightened world order such a connection would be spiritually fructifying, but intolerance, a narrow view of permissible sexual expression, and a universal deficiency in social imagination mean that such a relationship, if it is pursued, can only end in tragedy. For March, convention and passion are locked in a conflict which no sort of compromise can resolve. Death is the only outcome possible for an absolute situation of this sort in which the intelligence proves ineffectual. The passion that burns between them is more negative than positive. After their quarrel Cocoanut bites his lover's arm brutally, as if to invite violence from Lionel. Lionel then takes him brutally, hardly conscious of what he is doing. He accompanies the frenzied sexual embrace with the act of strangulation and thereafter rushes overboard to his death.

Lionel's mother, an asexual Victorian matriarch who would have disowned Lionel had he been involved in a sexual scandal, is a figure of evil portent in the background. Her possessiveness which lacks the excuse of sexual passion may well be the greatest perversion of all, although there is nothing illicit about it. She represents at one level all the frightening power of tradition which punishes remorselessly those who fail to respect accepted norms for social behavior; she is also the castrating female, the enemy of all passion, but the enemy in particular of atypical passion. The subtleties and ramifications of the relationships between Lionel and Cocoanut are balanced then by those between Lionel and his mother and by the strong enmity that Mrs. March and Cocoanut have always felt toward each other. In the story, the homosexual relationship has implications that extend to the universal; it is only the dominating strand in a tale that has many thematic threads. Forster is especially preoccupied with exploring the tensions in passionate relationships between possessiveness and the compulsion to restrict the freedom of the beloved on the one hand and the need for the beloved to experience complete freedom and trust on the other hand, if such relationships are to stand a chance of surviving.

The best of the later stories represent with authority Forster as a keen social observer, as an ironic commentator on manners and morals, as an analyst of human motives, and as a portrayer of character. Romance elements, especially hints of the supernatural and an intense struggle between the powers of good and evil, are often forcefully present. The involutions of the psyche, the nearness of the extraordinary (or the supernatural) to the ordinary, and the shifting lines that exist between an objectively stated reality and its symbolical ramifications are the principal characteristics of Forster's more important later tales as they are of his earlier tales and his novels. The best stories in *The Life to Come* reveal a genius in mature control of the powers that had already reached their fullest fruition in the novels. They throw unexpected shafts of light upon the characters and the situations in these novels, though the novels should not be interpreted solely within the sexual framework provided by these tales.

Chapter Six

"A Universe . . . not . . . Comprehensible to Our Minds": *A Passage to India*

Genesis of "Passage";
Forster as Comic Ironist

The general judgment can stand that *A Passage to India* is Forster's best novel.[1] More than in his other works, Forster reveals a disciplined intelligence, an intellectual consistency, an expertise of craftsmanship, a firm design, a full articulation of a complex vision, a subtlety of thought, and a breadth of view that results in a memorable evocation of empire and the Indian subcontinent.

India had enkindled Forster's mind as a result of his friendship with Syed Ross Masood, "who showed me new horizons and a new civilisation," even before he visited there for the first time in 1912–1913.[2] When he got to India, its enigmatic aspect grasped his imagination, and as he later said of his experience in Dewas, "It was the great opportunity of my life."[3] Not only did Indian civilization cast its spell over him, but the clash of cultures and modes of life, of temperaments and values, appealed to him as writer. He began a novel in 1913, using Bankipore or Patna as the original for the city of Chandrapore, the adjacent Barabar Hills as the model for the Marabar, and the principalities of Dewas and Chhatarpur as the prototypes for the Mau of the concluding sequence. In the main he drew upon his friends Masood, Abu Saeed Mirza, and the Maharajah of Dewas State Senior for Aziz and upon two Maharajahs, of Dewas State Senior and of Chhatarpur, for

Godbole. Fielding, as Stallybrass thinks, was probably a compound of Forster himself and his Anglo-Indian friend in the government service, Sir Malcolm Darling; Ralph Moore, as Furbanks suggests, embodies some aspects of the earlier Forster; and Mrs. Moore can be mostly viewed as a reworking of Ruth Wilcox of *Howards End*.[4]

Forster had difficulty in completing the novel after he had begun to envisage the Marabar Caves episode; he interrupted work on the novel to write *Maurice*, and then the war intervened. His life as Red Cross volunteer in Alexandria during the war, however, helped sharpen Forster's apprehension of civilizations different from those of Western Europe, the affair with Mohammed el Adl underlay the warm friendship between Aziz and Fielding, and the Alexandrian interlude extended his knowledge of the relationships between Britain and subject countries.[5] He was not able to resolve the novel, until after his second visit to India, of ten months in 1921–1922, as private secretary to the Maharajah of Dewas State Senior and until after he had participated there in the festivities celebrating the birth of the Indian god, Shri Krishna. This festival, he said, was "the strangest and strongest Indian experience ever granted me."[6] On Forster's return to England Leonard Woolf's encouragement was crucial, as was the inspiration provided by a reading of Marcel Proust. *A Passage to India* appeared in 1924 to general acclaim, though some controversy developed concerning Forster's treatment of Anglo-Indian officials.[7]

One chief strain in the earlier work, that of ironical comedy, is present in *A Passage to India*, but the comedy deepens to achieve a metaphysical significance mostly latent in the preceding novels. Ostensibly, Forster explored the relationships between the English administrators of empire and the Indian people they controlled. He presented the Anglo-Indian officials—Turton, Heaslop, McBryde, Major Callendar—and their womenfolk satirically, but other English people such as Mrs. Moore and Fielding he treated with sympathy. The reverent Mrs. Moore impresses Doctor Aziz, the mercurial Moslem, almost in spite of himself when he encounters her at night in the mosque at Chandrapore. Mrs. Moore is in India as

companion to Adela Quested, who is likely to become engaged
to Ronny Heaslop, one of the ruling Anglo-Indians and Mrs.
Moore's son. Aziz invites the two ladies, the Hindu educator
Godbole, and Fielding, the British principal of the local Indian
college, to a picnic at the Marabar Caves, several miles distant
from Chandrapore. In the Caves Mrs. Moore undergoes a total
disillusionment; and Adela experiences either panic or hallu-
cination and accuses Aziz of sexual assault.

The last half of the book traces the repercussions of this
incident and of Adela's retraction of her charges against Aziz,
under the influence of the now dead Mrs. Moore. The latter
had departed earlier from India because her presence there had
become an embarrassment to her son, Ronny, and she dies on
board ship. Aziz is set free when Adela withdraws her accusa-
tion against him, but the Anglo-Indians still believe in his guilt.
He feels, moreover, that Fielding has betrayed him by helping
the honest but misguided Adela to endure her unpopularity
among the British after she refuses to participate in the pros-
ecution of Aziz. Thereafter, he retires to the princely state of
Mau, where Godbole has preceded him. On a trip to India
Fielding visits Mau with his wife (the former Stella Moore) and
his brother-in-law, Ralph Moore. Under the influence of the
Shri Krishna ceremonies and of the spiritual presence of Mrs.
Moore, Fielding and Aziz achieve a tentative reconciliation
before cultural and political differences once again part them.
Mrs. Moore had achieved an Indian immortality by being
transformed at the time of Aziz's trial into "Esmiss Esmoor, a
Hindu goddess," and she is reincarnated in the children of her
second marriage, Ralph and Stella. Aziz can even write to
Adela thanking her for her courage in exonerating him at the
trial, and he wishes now to do nothing but "kind actions all
round and wipe out the wretched business of the Marabar for
ever." [8] Henceforth, he will associate her with a name "very
sacred" to him, that of Mrs. Moore.

Ironic detachment, controlled satire, and an appreciation of
comic incongruities inform Forster's presentation of social,
imperial, and racial issues. "The bridge party" at the British
Club, which Turton arranges for Miss Quested and Mrs.
Moore, reveals Forster as a comic writer alive to the tragic

meaning of racial misunderstanding. The failure of the party to "bridge" the races is ironic, and Mrs. Turton's rudeness to her native guests has sinister, as well as ludicrous overtones. Her advice to Adela Quested and Mrs. Moore—to remember that they are "superior to everyone in India except one or two of the Ranis, and they're on an equality" (42)—comments implicitly on her arrogance and her limited sympathies; and Forster in his description of her use of Urdu ("to speak to her servants, so she knew none of the politer forms and of the verbs only the imperative mood," 42) is the witty satirist who conveys implicitly the spiritual deficiencies of the English rulers of India.

Only after Aziz's imputed sexual insolence has roused the English community does Forster reveal fully his powers as sardonic commentator upon a tense social situation. The irony is both verbal and dramatized. At this point, Forster describes with asperity Adela's effect on the Anglo-Indians as bringing out "all that was fine in their character" (179); and Adela herself is subject to ironic scrutiny when Forster views the resumption of "her morning kneel to Christianity" as indicating her desire to be reassured that "God who saves the King will surely support the police" (211).

The ironies inherent in the situations are manifold. The subaltern at the club praises the Indian with whom he has recently played polo without knowing that the prisoner he condemns is this same man. Then, too, the questions arising from Adela's case loom so much greater to the English than do her misfortunes that inevitably her countrymen forget her as a person. Police Superintendent McBryde prosecutes Aziz by acting on his theory that all people born south of thirty degrees latitude are "criminals at heart." But he has been having an affair with Miss Derek and is guilty of a transgression similar to the one for which he prosecutes an innocent man. The farcical intrudes when the English are ordered from the platform of the courtroom to which they had removed when Adela needed air. The Anglo-Indians experience outrage because they sense a loss to their prestige in having to obey the timorous request of the native magistrate. Always in this novel, distinctive modulations both in style and substance occur that reveal the presence of the dispassionate yet sympathetic analyst of human inconsistencies and of corruptions to which the exercise of power can lead.

Although some have criticized Forster for his unfairness to the Anglo-Indians, Benita Parry in *Delusions and Discoveries: Studies on India in the British Imagination 1880–1930* (1972) has demonstrated that former novelists about India, including even Kipling, had subscribed to the racism, the sexual hysteria, and the political intolerance that Forster satirized in *A Passage to India*. Suffice to say that Ronny Heaslop and the other exemplars of empire represent a complex of ideas that does violence to the culture of India as an independent entity. According to G. K. Das, the author of *Forster's India*, this complex of ideas comprised "the Burkean doctrine of imperial trusteeship, the utilitarian doctrine of state activity propounded mainly by Bentham and the two Mills, the Platonic idea of a ruling elite to act as wise guardians, and the Evangelical belief in the spread of the gospel for the benefit of all heathens." [9] Such a combination of forces in control would leave little room for Indian culture to breathe, let alone flourish. The guardian concept, in particular, invested an absolute power in British officials that they could easily abuse. Recent commentators have also revealed that *Passage* is a political document, with implicit and explicit references to the Amritsar Massacre of 1919, the *Khilafat* (pro-Turkey) Moslem movement after the war, the unsteady relationship between Hindus and Moslems that culminated in the violence between them after World War II, and the emerging nationalist noncooperation movement of the 1920s. [10]

The "Double Vision" and the Tentative Hindu Synthesis

A Passage to India is important for its social and political implications and for its revelations of Forster's luminous intelligence. Nevertheless, the book's appeal is primarily aesthetic, symbolic, and philosophic. Forster's creative imagination, as it illuminated the elemental aspects of humanity, results in this novel's richness. Forster saw his book as metaphysical rather than social in impact since he "tried to indicate the human predicament in a universe which is not, so far, comprehensible to our minds."[11] The book exists chiefly as a vibrant aesthetic entity which comments implicitly upon issues that are universal in their significance. In its approach to the transcendent *A Passage to India* reaches romance and prophecy, but it does so without sacrifice of social verisimilitude.

The "double vision," which bridges the extremities of existence, expresses Forster's main preoccupation in *A Passage to India*. He conjoined opposites as he had done earlier; but in *A Passage to India* the mediation is more an ongoing process for which only tentative resolutions exist. The exertions of the individual's will are important; so is the quality of the individual's mind and sensibility. For the superficial individual, guided only by his intellect, the possibility of attaining unity will not occur, or it will seem unimportant. Only an individual with developed powers of intuition can grasp the polarities of experience and see them in their true relationships.

When such polarities are continually present to the consciousness, truth is paradoxical. So throughout the book Forster stresses the complex qualities of ultimate reality and of God, and his attitude toward nature and the primitive is also complicated. He communicates the ambivalence of the Marabar Caves and the Gokul Ashtami festival; and he conveys, too, the elusive quality of Godbole, the individual who most often expresses a convoluted view of reality or dramatizes it in his conduct. Mrs. Moore is, moreover, at once a woman who is repelled by life in India and one who grasps its essence.

Godbole's Hinduism takes us beyond good and evil to a cosmic force more often passive than positive and always unpredictable. At Fielding's party Professor Godbole explains that his song is a lament for the God who does not come; and, in reply to Mrs. Moore, he explains further that no song exists that celebrates His certain coming. Following the disaster at the Marabar Caves, Godbole is even more explicit, if still exasperating, to Fielding. "Absence implies presence," Godbole says, though the two are not the same. Yet absence is not "non-existence," so we can say, "Come, come, come, come," in the hope that at some time the Divine may descend. Just as

absence and presence are related, so are good and evil as aspects
of the Divine. Both together, not either one separately, express
the total universe. To desire the one without acknowledging
the power of the other is to falsify. In the Caves Mrs. Moore is,
unwittingly, the victim of simplified notions. She is immobi-
lized because she finds God in His absent aspect when she had
been too eager for God in His present aspect. Godbole, on the
other hand, knows God's presence in "Temple" because he is
less anxious to find Him and because he perceives that God will
inevitably soon again be absent from him. Godbole is, in short,
mystically more sophisticated than his English counterpart,
Mrs. Moore.

Evil is not to be desired but to be endured, since its presence
presupposes also the existence of good which will in its turn
dominate. Good and evil are also universal human characteristics. When an evil act is performed, everyone has done it,
Godbole asserts. So, if Adela were affronted in the cave,
everyone who knew her shares complicity, whether or not he
was present. Even Adela is in part guilty, as she sometimes
senses when she heeds her deepest instincts instead of her
intellect.

Godbole is a reconciling agent, wise but passive, intense yet
indifferent. His mien suggests an imperturbable confidence,
the result both of effort and of effortless vision: ". . . his whole
appearance suggested harmony—as if he had reconciled the
products of East and West, mental as well as physical, and
could never be discomposed" (72). He also has a preternatural
insight which none of the other characters possesses, except in
part Mrs. Moore. Like his fellow Hindus, Godbole continually seeks the unseen, a chief aspect of the Hindu temperament as
Forster elsewhere described it: "The Hindu is concerned not
with conduct, but with vision. To realize what God is seems
more important than to do what God wants. He has a constant
sense of the unseen—of the powers around if he is a peasant, of
the power behind if he is a philosopher, and he feels that this
tangible world, with its chatter of right and wrong, subserves
the intangible." [12] One who beholds the beatific vision can,
like Godbole, die to the world and refuse to act in conformity
to social pressures; one who beholds the horrific vision can,

like Mrs. Moore, die to the world, refuse to help her friends, and long for her own death.

Mrs. Moore, who misunderstands her vision at the Marabar, dies before she can see it in perspective. Alone, she is unable to reach the reality symbolized by the Hindu temple where all life forms merge: "life human and superhuman and subhuman and animal, life tragic and cheerful, cruel and kind, seemly and obscene." [13] At the temple's apex is the sun which expresses the unity underlying these forms and the unity to which they aspire. It is the underside of this unity that Mrs. Moore encounters in the Caves; and it is only in death that she attains the knowledge of all sides of it.

Her stature increases when she, at death, is transformed into an Indian presence with powers similar to, and possibly exceeding, Godbole's own. In mythic terms she becomes a goddess who saves Aziz at the trial, who brings the truth to Adela, who brings healing rains and fertility to the parched land by the sacrifice of her life, and who reconciles East and West through her surviving influence in the minds of Aziz and Godbole and in the personalities of her children, Ralph and Stella. This redemptive aspect of Mrs. Moore is consistent with her mystical sensitivity in the first pages of the book; but she must endure a spiritual crucifixion before she can exert transcendent power. She is buried in the ocean before she becomes a Hindu goddess, just as the image of Shri Krishna must be thrown into the Mau tank before He can exert His remaining strength. As one critic suggests, Mrs. Moore atones for the rape of India by her countrymen through saving the life of an Indian accused of assaulting an English woman. [14]

Godbole does not figure greatly in the action, but he is the chief source of truth as the representative of the most comprehensive world view in the novel, that of Hinduism. Hinduism enables Godbole to divine the complex relationships between himself and an unseen power beyond the here and now. Fact to Hinduism is less important than the intangible, as Forster had seen in 1914: "Greece, who has immortalized the falling dust of facts, so that it hangs in enchantment for ever, can bring no life to a land that is waiting for the dust to clear away, so that the soul may contemplate the soul." [15] Forster's own allegiance was divided: as a scion of G. E. Moore, Grecian fact remained for him an indispensable component of the spiritual life, but as a visionary, sensitive to the mystical philosophy of Plotinus and that of the Orient, the lure of the Hindu venture into the spiritual world also exerted its spell.

If Godbole provided him with some of his standards, still Forster did not accept Hinduism uncritically. Its philosophical drift interested him more than its external aspects; like Mrs. Moore's children, Ralph and Stella, he was drawn to Hinduism but unconcerned about its forms. On balance, Hinduism meant more to him than either Islam or Christianity. In *The Hill of Devi* (127) he commended Islam for its order and criticized Hinduism for its disorder. But in the 1960s he could disparage Islam for its "orderliness." [16] In the novel he asserted that "the shallow arcades" of the mosque do not take us very deep into religious mysteries nor does Islam's primary belief, "There is no God but God"; and he referred scornfully to the "poor, talkative Christianity" that had been Mrs. Moore's solace before she entered the Marabar Caves.

Forster revealed a still more positive affinity with Hinduism when he described himself on "nearer nodding terms with Krishna than with any other god," and when he perceived the power of Hinduism over skeptical temperaments such as his own: "it has caught sceptics at all times, and wrings cries of acquiescence and whispers of hope." [17] In Hinduism Forster found an encompassing reality that could unify the world and bind together animate and inanimate life, an impersonal spiritual force with which one might identify mystically, and a belief in love as a binding spiritual and moral value—a "love in which there neither was nor desired to be sensuality, though it was excited at the crisis and reached ecstasy." [18]

The Marabar Caves: "Illusion . . . Set Against the Background of Eternity"

The Marabar Caves embody the neutral substratum of the universe and lack positive attributes. [19] Just as Hinduism takes us philosophically to a plane beyond good or evil, so the Caves exist physically—insofar as natural objects can—in a void, having been created before space and time began. They contain, therefore, a primordial reality, basic to all later differentiations of being, animate or inanimate, in space or time. Godbole intuitively knows this truth about the Caves, but at Fielding's tea party he senses that his Moslem and Occidental audience would not understand him if he were now to describe it. Godbole realizes that in the Caves one may have perceptions which reach "straight back into the universal, to a blackness and sadness so transcending our own that they are undistinguishable from glory."[20] In these words, whereby Forster expresses the concern of Melville and other prophetic writers, he characterizes the intuitions of Godbole, the formidable negations experienced by Mrs. Moore in the Marabar, and the affirmations she fails to find there.

If the inmost Caves were to be excavated, nothing would be added to the sum of good and evil, Forster explains; yet good and evil, and all other polarities, are in the Caves.[21] The reality the Caves enclose can extend in a negative or a positive direction as circumstances or the powers of the individual permit. They were created before pestilence or treasure, Forster says; but pestilence and treasure, and all such contrarieties, develop from them.

The Caves and Hills are genuinely extraordinary and their meaning is elusive. Close at hand they present "a nasty little cosmos"; at a distance, they seem finite and romantic and breathe a promise of spiritual renewal. Everything in the world possesses equal value, the Caves assert through their confounding echo; and there is nothing special, then, about man and his aspirations. If man is equal to all other beings, he has no special value in himself but is as valuable as all other manifestations of existence, valuable as a wasp, a snake, or a sun-burnt rock. He is not necessarily at the apex of a great chain of being nor a little less than the angels. Godbole knows that the world was not made for man, but Mrs. Moore's Christianity does not allow her to see that far.

Fearsome as the Caves are in their aboriginal darkness, when a light is struck the beauties of the reflected light are like "exquisite nebulae." What had seemed completely dark is the source of light; and the Caves, with their rough exterior surface, possess hidden beauty. The struggling of the flames within the granite walls to reach the source of light on the outside is symbolic of the efforts of Godbole, Mrs. Moore, and some of the others to let their human fires merge with a divine fire. And the radiance increases as image and flame seemingly touch each other and "kiss" before they expire, just as the soul expires when in Hinduism it merges with the world soul to achieve its Nirvana.

The powers of nullity are too strong for the English women to withstand at the Marabar. The Caves overwhelm them, saddling Mrs. Moore with disillusion and Adela with delusion. There, the eternal and the infinite lack beauty and sublimity, and become ugly and sinister. The unseen achieves expression not only in the unsettling echo but in such a phenomenon as the cheeping of the mangy squirrel outside Aziz's house before the picnic. During the hot weather at least, the infinite has no link with exaltation, aesthetic or spiritual. The two women feel isolated from other people and from each other; and the Caves intensify and bring to focus their latent frustrations: Mrs. Moore's doubts about her usefulness as a human being and Adela's misgivings about sex and love.

The concept of eternity becomes equivalent in the Caves to an "undying worm," and this worm or serpent is full of crawling maggots. Insofar as the serpent is a phallic emblem of the life principle, it is contorted and twisted in the Caves; life, as seen from the perspective of the Caves, recoils on itself and has no purposeful motion. Even Shri Krishna, a life-god in Hinduism, had once appeared as a fearsome serpent to churn the seas in order to form the objects of creation and to interchange them so as to cause them to lose their individuality.[22] To Mrs. Moore, life, seen purposefully, retreats before the echo's expression of chaos, disorder, and negation. As yet, she has no power to see that chaos and disorder betoken life as well as death, and imply, by their very existence, the existence of their opposites. Men can endure only so much of the negation that Mrs. Moore finds in the echo before they retreat into the self, where they are apt to find all too little strength. The echo muffles Mrs. Moore's spirit, just as a direct view of God might have blinded her.[23]

The unseen is sinister only when it confronts one starkly. If, as Fielding says, "the echo is always evil," that which the echo emanates from need not be. If one penetrates the echo, he may not be totally reassured; but he will, likely as not, find a reality that is more than negative. But reality remains hidden and can only be grasped evanescently, even by the adept. Preparatory to her visit to the Caves Mrs. Moore sees the universe as a series of receding arches with an echo beyond the last arch, and then a silence. The silence is evidently Eternity, impassive but not hostile; the echo in its reverberation is more malign than the silence. The wise man accepts the universe as it is; and he sees that its apparent evils, if overpowering, need not be permanent. Arch and echo are expanding and retracting images that connect the individual, sometimes against his will, with an Eternity more ominous than reassuring. Yet the existence of the Eternal, however veiled to human eyes, argues for a measure of stability and meaning in a chaotic universe.

Fielding and Adela do not understand the mysteries inherent in the Hills or the terrors inherent in the Caves, but they do have glimmers of perception. The Anglo-Indians, who have none at all, are unequal to India and think, for example, that its irrational energies can be controlled by numbering the Marabar Caves with paint to distinguish one from another. The antagonism between Ronny and his mother, particularly after Aziz's arrest, indicates his failure to comprehend the irrational forces that now sway her.

Ronny is not at home anywhere in India, in mosque, caves, or temple ("Mosque," "Caves," and "Temple" are, in fact, the titles of the three successive divisions of the novel). He is symbolic of the rootless Anglo-Indian officials who lack not only Mrs. Moore's mystical awareness, but Fielding's graciousness and humanity, Adela's sincerity, and Aziz's dedication to the personal. Those who attend Fielding's tea party would not be misfits in the "Mosque," but they would not understand (except for Godbole) the full implications of "Caves" or "Temple."

The Caves comprise the sum total of all experience—the locus of community activity and of burial rites, the womb and tomb of all existence, an archetype of the great mother and of annihilation.[24] In the Caves one can discern the upward swirl of aspiration and the downward pull of fact, the life in the unconscious and the failure of the mind to comprehend this life. The Caves include, besides, all the rhythms of existence, especially the most basic, that of life versus death. It is sometimes difficult to disentangle the life from the death principle. One implies the other, just as absence asserts presence, and evil, good. The Caves, which embody death as well as life, are of "very dead and quiet" granite; and Mrs. Moore receives one part of India's message, the disabling echo, in "that scoured-out cavity of the granite" (208). Rock is refractory, although as Forster implies elsewhere (247), stones, as well as plants and animals, feel perhaps the pain of the universe and are potentially sentient. In *Alexandria* Forster had said that for the Neoplatonist all things are parts of God, including the stones;[25] and he had implied, therefore, that some mystics had achieved a completeness greater than Godbole's. In Hinduism "completeness" matters, not "reconstruction," which may be too human in implication (286).

But even Professor Godbole cannot assimilate stones to his vision of cosmic unity though he can merge with Mrs. Moore, whom he only dimly remembers, and the wasp. The stones signify the difficulty in his attaining completeness of vision rather than, as one critic asserts, an inability to attain it.[26] Another fact emerges: the negations of the Marabar cannot be assimilated to a philosophy less inclusive than that symbolized by the Caves and Hills. Hinduism, alone of the religions presented, has the comprehensiveness to absorb such realities.

As many of the most perceptive commentators have suggested, the Caves relate to Hinduism. The presence of caves in Hindu myths and rituals, the correspondence between illusions (such as those experienced in the Marabar) and the Hindu veils of Maya, the similarity of the echo sound to that of the mystic syllable "om," and the presence of flame and serpent imagery alike at the Marabar and in Hindu scriptures link the Marabar Caves to Hinduism. One need not assert that Mrs.

Moore has a Hindu vision there; rather she undergoes, as Forster said, "the vision . . . with its back turned." [27] The revelation to her is less a repudiation of Hinduism, however, than an apprehension of the negative aspect of its primal reality.

If the Caves embody a life principle however contorted or disguised or remote from us, they also suggest the death principle. After too great an exposure to the forces let loose at the Marabar, the characters return to Chandrapore in a train that seems dead though it moves; and all the people in it are like corpses. The Hills are seen as gods, and the earth is a ghost in comparison. So, as dwellers on the plain, we find that our mundane lives and values become illusory before the cosmic truth concentrated in the Hills; in their vicinity, "everything seemed cut off at its root, and therefore infected with illusion" (140).

Forster also agreed with a statement which he quoted in a review and which stressed the insignificance of our lives when compared to the transcendent: ". . . for in Indian art, as in Indian philosophy, all life, even the life of the gods, is an illusion or play set against the background of eternity." [28] Such a juxtaposition of meaning and nothingness is too difficult for Mrs. Moore and the non-Hindus in the novel to grasp entire. The dispelling of illusion and the confronting of a first Reality should, for the initiated, eventuate in knowledge and insight rather than in the disillusion suffered by Mrs. Moore. All of Mrs. Moore's spiritual constructs—love, beauty, piety—now lack abiding force for her at the Marabar. They are man-made, abstract formulations, irrelevant to the amoral, primordial essence of things, revealed both in the Caves and in Hinduism.

The Hills—and by implication the Caves which they cover—overwhelm by excess; they lack the "proportion" seen even in the most rugged hills elsewhere and deflect the aspiration for a comprehensible certitude. The Caves and the negations undergone there by the Western visitors are crucial. But the Caves open out to the Shri Krishna birth festivities and provide for their exuberance the most solid possible base. Just so the cave, with its suggestion of mystery and the elemental, is at the heart of the temple. But the cave is also subsumed by the entire temple which flaunts a multifaceted, inclusive rendition of outward forms. The antecedent matrix of being, contained in the Caves, is assimilated into the total structure of creation. It is never lost, however, and we must be prepared to acknowledge its violent, primitive effects. If Hinduism has inclusiveness, it is not orderly: "Ragged edges of religion . . . unsatisfactory and undramatic tangles . . . God si love" (316).

This amorphousness permits Hinduism to absorb disillusionment and apathy, as well as creativity and joy—both the experiences that transfigure life and the knowledge that these experiences are also illusions that perish. If the ceremonies possess "fatuity," they also possess "philosophy."[29] In its widest reaches Hinduism would annihilate sorrow for all: "not only for Indians, but for foreigners, birds, caves, railways, and the stars; all became joy, all laughter; there had never been disease nor doubt, misunderstanding, cruelty, fear" (288). Truly, as Forster said in 1914, in the Hindu view of things "the divine is so confounded with the earthly that anyone or anything is part of God."[30] If the Caves induce in the unprepared individual a dynamic nihilism, the Temple festivities induce in the prepared individual a sense of cosmic unity and of dynamic life.

A "Bewildering . . . Echoing Contradictory World"

The structure of the novel illustrates its paradoxical content. Many readings, however, stress a "triadic" structure of thesis, acting upon antithesis, to produce a synthesis; and this kind of progression is not absent from the book.[31] The rational, sentimentalized views of God, such as the Moslem Aziz and the Christian Mrs. Moore express in "Mosque," crumble when an indifferent cosmos subdues Mrs. Moore and Adela Quested in "Caves." In turn, the spiritual lethargy induced by the Marabar and the evil forces of division let loose there yield partly in "Temple" to the mystical strengths of Hinduism, its emphasis upon love, and the breadth of its philosophy. Each section of the novel is, moreover, associated with one of the three principal seasons of the Indian year. [32] Still, the novel charts primarily the dualities of life as they exist in uneasy conjunction with one another rather than the transmutation of them into something else. All contrasting objects and mental states merge into the Unity underlying the universe, but they do not usually become something else midway in the process.

The motion of the novel is cyclic rather than linear; dialectical opposites are not resolved and continue indefinitely to exert their strength. Forster is at once preoccupied with a timeless unity and with the concrete manifestations of that unity in time. So at the end Aziz distrusts, then accepts, a cyclic explanation of his life; and he realizes that little enough has been resolved through his sufferings. His encounter with Ralph Moore induces a fear that the Mosque-Caves cycle may start again. He dreads the prospect but perceives that he cannot avoid the inevitable.

The dispelling of drought and suffering by the monsoon rains organizes the novel in terms of a cyclic fertility ritual, as Ellin Horowitz and other critics have suggested; and Mrs. Moore is, as we have seen, the god who must be sacrificed in order that the healing rains descend. In this cyclic pattern the progress is from affirmation to negation to qualified affirmation. Nothing is canceled. The forces of division and unity still exist, but in "Temple" they reveal themselves in a double aspect, as temporal and eternal. Temporal discordances will in time yield to a merging of hitherto abrasively active dichotomies.

In "Temple" the affirmation is tentative and hard-earned. Mrs. Moore's assertion, "God is Love," in "Mosque" had been too complacent. The Hindu version of this same principle, "God si Love," is more flexible; the fact that the Hindu recognizes mundane chaos is implied in the misspelling of the verb. For the Hindu, love is more abstract, more transcendental, more removed from the individual's desires and ideals than for the Christian or the Moslem. Though infinite love is the basis for the Hindu religion, the Hindu regards "love" apart from the order and the precise formulations of the Western or Islamic mind.

Love for the Hindu is an experience at once more immediate

and more remote, less fastidious and more far-reaching, than
for other men. For Godbole, and indeed for Mrs. Moore in her
mystical moments, love extends to the wasps and, by implication, to all forms of animate life; and Godbole would include
the inanimate, the stones of India, if he could manage to do so.
The progression of the book is from light to darkness to
modified light; the fact that illumination once existed implies
that it may come again: "Hope existed despite fulfilment, as it
will be in heaven" (303).

The nature of God Himself, as the Hindu envisages it, is
complex. In "Temple" Godbole is standing in the presence of
God but removed from Him, at the other end of a carpet which
distances Him from His worshipper. God, in short, exists; but
He is difficult to know. All statements about Him are alike true
and untrue: "He is, was not, is not, was" (283). God has not
yet been born when the Shri Krishna ceremonies begin; He
will be born at midnight, but He was also born centuries ago;
He can never be born, perhaps, because, as the Lord of the
Universe, He has always existed and transcends all human
endeavors to encompass Him in creed or in ritual. At the
height of the festivities He is thrown into the water; but He
can't be thrown away. Such are the ambiguous rituals that the
Hindu observes, such the certainties and uncertainties inherent
in all spiritual proceedings. The God to be thrown away and all
other such images and symbols are, Forster says, "emblems of
passage": "a passage not easy, not now, not here, not to be
apprehended except when it is unattainable" (314). [33] In any
event, God transcends the categories that we can formulate for
Him.

Nature, another manifestation of the unseen, is scarcely
amenable to the understanding. The Ganges River seems glam-
orous in the moonlight to Mrs. Moore when she first visits
India, but she recoils when she learns that crocodiles inhabit it.
Now the river seems both terrible and wonderful. "The "jolly" jungle scenery at Mau also conceals a deadly cobra, as Aziz
and Fielding go on their final ride; the scenery, though it
"smiles," places, as it were, a "gravestone on any human
hope" (321). If nature is apparently indestructible, she is yet
undergoing slow change and erosion; and gradually the plain

will engulf the hills which are of "incredible antiquity" and "flesh of the sun's flesh" (123).

Nature is not only an imponderable force but a vital, animating one, as Forster's personification of the Hills and his use of the pathetic fallacy in describing them indicate. The Hills both "lie flat" and "heave"; they "creep forward" to the city and "leap" to beauty at sunset; they thrust "fists and fingers" up to the sky; inside, the walls of the Caves are skin to the fists and fingers; and the foothills are "knees" to the other hills. The surrounding caves and boulders proclaim that they are alive; and when the intruders to the "queer valley" leave, "stabs" of hot air pursue them. If Grasmere is more manageable and more romantic than India, it is also less real and alive. Mrs. Moore, when she comes to India and sees the moon in all its splendor, thinks how dead and alien it had seemed to her in England.

The punkah wallah (fan attendant) at the trial is a symbol of India's natural vitality. Under his impassive influence Adela becomes aware of more than her own sufferings and is receptive to the double vision which awakens in her when the crowd outside the court chants its version of Mrs. Moore's name, "Esmiss Esmoor." The punkah wallah, as an embodiment of the Life-Force, contrasts with "the serpent of eternity" known in the Caves; Adela understands neither one fully, though each one disturbs her radically. The resplendent Indian who in "Temple" wades into the Mau tank during the tempest to consign the palanquin bearing Shri Krishna's image to the waves is, like the punkah wallah, an emblem of primitive strength.

The truth is that India is both a muddle and a mystery, but a mystery that can only be reached through muddle. So the Temple ceremonies are "a triumph of muddle," though they suggest certain transcendent truths. To those who experience her superficially, India seems vast and amorphous, a country where life abounds but where discernible purpose is absent: "There seemed no reserve of tranquillity to draw upon in India . . . or else tranquillity swallowed up everything" (78). To those who can penetrate the outward confusion, she proves to be a mystery and purveys certain truths. India's very size and multiple cultures prevent anyone from understanding her easi-

ly, let alone completely. The Indian countryside is too vast to
admit of excellence; only from the remotest perspective, from
the moon for instance, would India acquire at last a firm
outline.

At the same time, categories in India are rigid and defeat the
attempts made to bridge them: so "the bridge party" is a
failure, and the picnic at the Marabar a fiasco when Aziz
"challenged the spirit of the Indian earth, which tries to keep
men in compartments" (127). The country is divided between
Moslems and Hindus who do not understand one another; and
even Hinduism fragments into a hundred dissenting sects. The
numerous inflexible distinctions found in Indian life reinforce the impression of disunity and multiplicity produced by
the landscape, the confused social patterns, and the many
civilizations of the subcontinent.

Aziz's desire to encompass "the vague and bulky figure of a
mother-land" (268) in his conversation and in his poems is
mostly false, therefore, since his idea of the diversities and of
the unity to be found in India is inadequate. For the Moslem,
India can be perplexing; so Aziz's dead wife looks out from her
portrait on a "bewildering . . . echoing, contradictory world"
(117), and Aziz in Mau dismisses the Hindu festival as remote
from any sanctities of his own. The Indian culture and the
Indian mind also baffle the rationalistic Westerner, leaving him
"with the sense of a mind infinitely remote from ours—a mind
patriotic and sensitive—and it may be powerful, but with little
idea of logic or facts; we retire baffled, and, indeed, exas-
perated."[34] At no point, moreover, are the Westerners so
confused, disturbed, and fascinated as by Godbole's im-
promptu song at Fielding's tea party.

There is something equivocal and difficult about life in India
that the sands of the Suez Canal and the Mediterranean countries wipe out as soon as one leaves the waters of the Orient.
The Mediterranean civilization has escaped "muddle" and
attained a true harmony, "with flesh and blood subsisting"
(282). From such a "norm" we depart as soon as we leave the
Mediterranean, particularly if we leave it to the South where
the "monstrous" and "extraordinary" are most likely to con-
front us, in India and the Orient in general. Western humanism

is unable to explain India; it is too selective and too easily abashed by the stubborn facts. In India new categories are difficult to impose, intellectual discriminations are often impossible to make, the unaided powers of the mind are insufficient to comprehend a land so diverse. In India, as Forster says in *The Hill of Devi*, "everything that happens is said to be one thing and proves to be another" (93). In the East the harmonies of Western art and religion are replaced by the dissonances of Hindu music, the teeming "world-mountain" of the Indian temple, and the sounds and confusions of the Gokul Ashtami rituals. On the other hand, the forms of Occidental art are reassuring to the Western European; but, satisfying as they are for him, they yet represent only a partial view of reality.

The Gokul Ashtami festival represents a "frustration of reason and form" and a "benign confusion"; the participants reveal a "sacred bewilderment." No one knows precisely what happens, "whether a silver doll or a mud village, or a silk napkin, or an intangible spirit, or a pious resolution, had been born" (290). In "Temple" Forster made aesthetic use of chaos similar to Emily Brontë's use of it in *Wuthering Heights*.[35] Since, in Forster's view, Brontë implied more than she said, she had had recourse to "muddle, chaos, tempest" to enable her characters to achieve through it the greatest degree of expressiveness for their superhuman experiences. So only in confusion can the Hindu religious rituals and the collision of the boats in the Mau tank during the tempest attain their ineffable implications. For the Eastern sensibility, vitality is surely more important than beauty. The Eastern mentality senses that the disorder of the universe presupposes an ultimate order; the conventional Western moralist or religionist would impose his own order upon the universe instead of responding to the strong chaotic currents within it which go beyond mere negation or mere affirmation.

Imagery: "Irradiating Nature from Within"

The image patterns in *A Passage to India* unify the novel. More subtly and insistently than in the early fiction, the method is symphonic. The three masses of the novel accumulate force and meaning through a polyphonic mounting of themes and images which reverberate in the mind and achieve symbolic expansion for the novel as it develops. The resolution is one that opens out rather than contracts. In discussing D. H. Lawrence as a prophetic writer in *Aspects of the Novel*, Forster revealed his own affinities with him. Judging his greatness to be aesthetic rather than intellectual, Forster recognized that Lawrence is a writer, "irradiating nature from within, so that every colour has a glow and every form a distinctness which could not otherwise be obtained" (144). These irradiations in both Lawrence and Forster result in great part from the use of an imagery as evocative as that found in formal poetry.

In Forster's view, sound or song is a principal component of prophetic fiction. As if to illustrate that his own book might be prophetic, Forster's most compelling images are auditory, from the "terrible gong" struck in the Marabar to the exuberant noises at Mau to the sounds, at once ominous and vital, heard in "Mosque" and elsewhere. These sounds convey the intense activities of a teeming nation and hint at the eruptive forces lying just below the surfaces of Oriental life; and they herald the presence—or the absence—of the Eternal. As in Melville's books, Forster's own "prophetic song," expressed primarily through Godbole, "flows athwart the action and the surface morality like an undercurrent" (*Aspects of the Novel*, 138).

An imagery based upon the "four elements," earth (rock), air, fire (heat, sun), and water predominates and strengthens the impression that *A Passage to India* elaborates elemental themes—is, in a word, "prophetic." The ambiguity that typically characterizes human experience extends as well to the image patterns in *Passage*. The fires of the stars are friendly, the hills at Mau have many temples "like little white flames," the reflected flames in the polished granite walls of the Caves are the sole source of beauty there, and the "exquisite nebulae" of these flames connect with the torches that "star" the farther shore of the lake when the Krishna images are consigned to the water. Stars connect also with Mrs. Moore and her beneficent influence: we remember, for example, her early mystical raptures when she gazes at the heavens, the presence of the stars on the acquittal night when Fielding and Aziz discuss her reported death, and the name of her daughter, Stella. Genuine warmth, again, characterizes the Shri Krishna ceremonies over which "the friendly sun of the monsoons" intermittently prevails.

But the fire images have negative meaning as well. The Anglo-Indians at the time of Aziz's arrest are "fired" by their intolerance; Turton is "fused by some white and generous heat"; the image of the ethereal and defenseless Mrs. Blakiston remains in the minds of the ladies "like a sacred flame"; "a not unpleasant glow" pervades the Anglo-Indians as they make ready to defend the purity of their homes from outward menace. The picnic, arrest, and trial take place in April, "herald of horrors," when the sun returns to tropic lands "with power but without beauty" and when "irritability and lust" prevail. Mrs. Moore resents the "barrier of fire" that will keep her "bottled up" in the hot weather; she is a victim of heat prostration after she traverses India in May. At the Caves "films of heat" descend capriciously from the Kawa Dal and "a patch of field would jump as if it was being fried" (141); and the visitors enter the Caves with "the sun crashing on their backs" (146).

A similar complexity marks the references to the air, the earth, and the water. The air at night, especially in the first and third parts of the novel, is sweet, cool, and friendly; and it contrasts with the air at the Caves which feels "like a warm bath into which hotter water is trickling constantly" (150). But the air from the punkah wallah's fan at the trial sweeps Adela on to a proclamation of the truth and gives her courage; at the end of the book, the air is "thick with religion and rain" (298), ostensibly in harmony with human aspirations and the renewal of the earth's fertility; and the freshening gale brings the boats on the Mau tank crashing together and leads to the reconciliation of the Indians and the English.

The sky has also beauty and serenity which shade off at times into hostility. At the storming of the hospital after the trial when "the spirit of evil again strode abroad" (235), the earth and sky are "insanely ugly"; at the Caves the sky dominates and seems "unhealthily near." But, at the end, the beautiful sunset sky is reflected in the Mau water tank; and pleasing white clouds and purple hills in the distance give a tranquil setting for Fielding's last ride with Aziz. The over-spreading sky is a symbol of infinitude in space as the hills are a symbol of infinitude in time; both furnish vistas that terrify the mind but intrigue the imagination—arch following upon arch, through the immense vault where hang the stars to the endless space beyond. The new geology and the new astronomy of the nineteenth century find their unerring correlatives, then, in the Marabar Hills and in the reaches of the sky above them. The sky is all powerful and "settles everything," and it can express both unity and division. Depending on the changes that take place there, the earth below becomes fruitful or barren, lux-uriant or stony.

Similarly, the earth both nourishes and destroys. It is malig-nant at the Marabar Caves, which are in a desert wasteland where earth vaunts its strength in the granite rock of the hills. But the same earth nourishes the lush jungle at Mau with its "jolly" vegetation and park-like beauty. Even the parched land about Bombay does not seem so lifeless to Mrs. Moore as the Indian plain had seemed, because man and his "indestructible life" are not absent from it; now, she can view the country for what it is, not for the way it refracts her inner agonies to her. Earth, finally, is the nourishing mother who bestows "myriads of kisses" as she draws the water of the monsoon into her inmost being.

The water images suggest the ceaseless flux of life in India, and can betoken its potential horror or its possible gift of peace. At the Marabar Caves the sultry atmosphere that feels like hot water has been mentioned; also, when one enters a cave, he is sucked into it like water going down a drain. Adela remembers that "the pale masses of the rock [at the Marabar] flowed round her" (228) as an enveloping flood and that the echo in the Caves "had spouted after her when she escaped, and was going on still like a river that gradually floods the plain" (194). The floods may also act as a divisive factor.

But, generally, the rains relieve the drought and are a friend-ly if primordial force. The festival flows on as a collective activity, potentially uniting all men; on the waters of the tank, the boats collide, and their occupants (Aziz and Ralph Moore, Fielding and Stella Moore) are thrown together to be reconciled as the tray bearing Krishna's image strikes the boats. The tray next comes near Godbole, who, a kind of magician, has presided over the ceremonies and the accident. To indicate his unity with both the human and divine, with the mundane and the transcendent, he smears upon his forehead some of the remaining mud from which the sacred images on the tray had been fashioned. The kissing sounds of the bats at the tanks also connote the healing effects exuding from the waters. Water also acts as a uniting symbol through the various tanks in the novel, one at each important locale: at the Mosque, at Fielding's garden, at the Marabar Caves, and at Mau. The tanks imply that in basic ways the races of mankind are one: physically, water satisfies a universal need; and, spiritually, when used in baptismal rites or other sacramental rituals, it also binds the races of man.

Intelligence versus Intuition: Forster's Characters

The chief characters in the novel, other than Godbole, are seen in terms of their reactions to the Marabar and the Gokul Ashtami festival; but they also exist powerfully as human beings. The Caves and the Temple ceremonies symbolize, respectively, the destructive and the creative forces underlying our life in society and in nature. They also represent the unconscious and its complexities; and, to the degree the individual comprehends the Caves and Temple, he achieves wholeness. Response to the truths of the unconscious is, however, often disappointing, for as Wilfred Stone states in a brilliant critique of *Passage*, "Consciousness and unconsciousness pursue each other in the novel, but they do not meet—and therein lies the world tragedy." [36] And, when they do meet, they meet to part, except as the individual can look forward with the years to an increased sense of the true proportions of life or to religious transfiguration. Quite simply, we do not achieve often enough for our spiritual well-being the fusion of will and creative power, of sense impressions and vision, of abstraction and prophecy. Of the characters, only Mrs. Moore and Godbole strain notably toward the mythic and the archetypal and reach the deepest sources of unconscious knowledge. The others move within fixed outlines of their preconceptions, the nuances of which, however, are defined in relationship to the mythic and elemental aspects of the book.

Aziz, regarded by critics as Forster's most brilliant creation, is contradictory and complicated; and he is the only exhaustively developed character. He is sensitive rather than responsive, but sensitive in a self-centered way, sensitive almost to the point of paranoia. He inclines, therefore, to suspicion rather than to trust; and his relationship with Fielding deteriorates when he suspects the Englishman of love for Adela Quested (thus Aziz explains Fielding's plea after the trial that he give up suing Adela for damages). Aziz, motivated by "the secret understanding of the heart," is far more spontaneous in his relationships than is Fielding, but this spontaneity misleads because it is uncritical. Although his "adoration" of Mrs. Moore runs deep, he is capable of cruelty to her son Ralph because of his own abstract hatred for the English and his unjust disappointment in Fielding. Like the earlier Mrs. Moore, Aziz is something of a romantic and attains his vision of harmony too readily, as he drops off to sleep and dreams of his joys flourishing without hindrance in "an eternal garden." Although he is mostly a figure whose strength is realistic, he does have the mythic dimensions suggested by Horowitz:[37] he is regarded by the Anglo-Indians as a demon lover and as a "dark rapist" of a violated virgin or white goddess.

The Western intellect, like the Moslem, is inadequate for an understanding of the Marabar—of truths reached by intuition. Aziz and Fielding are rationalists, despite Aziz's emotional nature and Fielding's magnanimity. Both men need the mellowing that mystical experience alone can give; they remain distrustful of the intuitive, although they achieve their best moments through its means. After the arrest when Fielding goes against the Anglo-Indians to defend Aziz, he feels a momentary affinity with the supernatural forces concentrated in the Hills; and, as a result of his wife's interest in Hinduism, he feels their union is "blessed" at last. Aziz, we remember, is at his most admirable when he recalls the profound Mrs. Moore and abandons the petty side of his nature.

Fielding senses the reality of India more accurately than Adela Quested, his compatriot; he sees it as a manifold entity and advises the credulous Adela to get to know Indians rather than India. As a humanist, he believes in reason; and for him the clarity of intellect is a primary value. He is a Bloomsbury intellectual let loose in India; and as such, he dislikes the muddle which he sees everywhere. The insistent mystery of India usually makes him uncomfortable.

About his rational values, Fielding continually has misgivings that disturb him. After his repudiation of Ronny Heaslop at the club, he looks at the Hills and perceives, despite the order he has imposed on his life, that something is missing from it and that he may never find out what. Hints of a mystical view of the world, which he cannot fully probe, visit him; we exist, he thinks, only in terms of each other's minds, though this is not a logical premise. He wants to discover the "spiritual side" of Hinduism, although he pursues this inquiry too intellectually; and he wishes to comprehend, perhaps too directly, the mystical elements in his wife's personality.

As descendants of the visionary Mrs. Moore, Stella and Ralph share their mother's sensitivity to the ineffable. Fielding knows that Stella aspires to kinds of insight he does not fully understand. Under the influence of Hinduism Stella attains calm and transfers some of it to Fielding. Their union is now strengthened because the "link outside either participant," needed for a firm relationship, has been forged. Their union thus represents a true marriage of the rational and the intuitive.

Reconciliation is still possible in this life, despite the sundered relationship between Aziz and Fielding—the "tragic separation of people who part before they need, or who part because they have seen each other too closely."[38] The parting involves a salutary recognition, by Aziz and Fielding, of this truth: the courage needed to face the inevitable may well be the quality needed to unite people. The "not yet" of the last paragraph implies an opposite state: a future fruition and union. The temple door shuts as the men take their last ride, implying an end of the concord between them; yet the door will some time open again and the divisions of daily life will then be transcended. Stella Moore in these pages is, like her mother, a wise priestess. To Fielding, she pronounces that the Marabar is wiped out, as a result of the boat collision; and Aziz emphasizes this truth by using the same words when he writes his letter to Adela. The reconciliation in the last pages is real but incomplete.

As a human being, Fielding is interesting and admirable; and one must agree with Thomson that "the limited achievement" of Fielding and Adela counts for more than their failures.[39] Fielding, a humanist, believes in the power of "good will plus culture and intelligence." If an excess of clarity is his flaw, he uses his reason to disarm the herd instinct and to combat the psychology of the mob. He is both "hard-bitten" and "good tempered"; and, if he lacks religious sensibility and recoils from open emotional display, he has tact and social imagination. He is popular with his students, he stays with the Indians at the bridge party, and he removes most of the obstacles to free discourse between himself and the typical Indian, Aziz. His flexible intelligence and his respect for ideas render him unpopular with those exponents of a rigid intellect, the Anglo-Indians. Although Fielding may be cynical about such relationships as marriage, his cynicism is superficial. It does not deter him from marriage or from conscientiousness in his ties with others. He is truly, as he says, a "holy man minus the holiness," a kind man suspicious of the ecstatic; and he travels somewhat less "light" than he thinks he does.

Adela Quested is excessively intellectual and humorless, too abstract in temper to attain profundity. She believes conscientiously in the sanctity of human relationships and tries sincerely to establish rapport with others. But such efforts derive from the will instead of the heart, so that she is unable to give effective expression to her ideals. She has an absolute honesty but lacks the imagination to render her honesty notable. She thus perceives that she was wrong to substitute tenderness, respect, and personal liking for love in her relationship with Ronny.

The experience in the Marabar Caves is crucial for Adela.

On the surface of her mind she thinks that Aziz is guilty: "the echo flourished, raging up and down like a nerve in the faculty of her hearing, and the noise in the cave, so unimportant intellectually, was prolonged over the surface of her life" (194). But when she gets beyond reason, she sees her actions more truly than when she thinks about them; and, in Mrs. Moore's real or imagined presence, the echo lessens or disappears. In Adela's moment of vision at the trial she sees her situation in both its present and its eternal aspect; and she momentarily attains wholeness. The day at the Marabar now seems one of "indescribable splendor"; and Adela pierces through to the other side of her delusion to see it truly. She achieves a doubleness of vision which enables her to realize that in any fundamental sense Aziz could not be guilty of rape. She now judges Aziz for what he is, not in terms of racial prejudice.

As for Mrs. Moore, she identifies herself at first too easily with the infinite. In her "itch for the seemly," she finds it difficult to acknowledge that mystical experience can be violent rather than serene, Dionysian rather than Apollonian. As one who desires "that joy shall be graceful and sorrow august and infinity have a form" (211), she is undone by India's sheer vitality, size, and age. On her way from India she perceives, however, that her nihilism may have been mistaken. As she sails home the palms at Asirgarh wave to her and proclaim that the Marabar was not final nor the echo there all of India. She fails as woman until too late to see this truth; but, as a Hindu goddess after her death, she exerts the spiritual force that had eluded her as a woman. If Mrs. Moore had in some crises been ineffective, she is nevertheless immortal as she survives into the memory of all who knew her. She has affected the innermost nature of one man, Aziz, who hears the notes of his salvation at the trial "Esmiss Esmoor" repeated in the interstices of the "Radhakrishna" song at the Mau festivities.

Mrs. Moore's fate in India seems similar to that of certain earlier Europeans who were more sympathetic to the Indians than most Anglo-Indians now are. For it was once possible for any mortal to become "not a whole god . . . but part of one, adding an epithet or gesture to what already existed, just as the gods contribute to the great gods, and they to the philosophic Brahm" (257). She has achieved, moreover, a completion in death—in the World Soul—that had evaded her in life. Her redemptive, goddess-like aspect has already been mentioned; and, in this aspect of her being, she is a "great mother" or "Kali" figure.[40] She is a tutelary genius for the book, since through Ralph and Stella she has been able to influence Fielding and Aziz and since Adela owes so much to her. Upon these persons her effects are convincing precisely because they have been won at such great expense, by a process involving not only the regeneration of others but her own death. Through her death she infuses renewed life: she thus symbolically projects the most compelling antithesis in this multifaceted book.

Chapter Seven

"Unexplored Riches and Unused Methods of Release": Nonfictional Prose and General Estimate

Forster's reputation rests chiefly on his novels, but his other writings are important. They make definite the ideas embedded in the novels, and they give firm expression to the liberal humanism. Some of the prose appeared before *A Passage to India*, but most of it came after his final novel. The only way after 1924 that he was able to comment on an unfamiliar world, he found, was through the less demanding forms of biography, the travel sketch, the personal essay, and the expository and critical treatise. Each of the volumes since 1924 has added significantly to the Forster canon, though not so boldly as another novel would have. Still, Forster's work would be less rich if he had ceased writing after 1924.

These books are important for what they reveal about Forster's ideas and intellectual preferences—and more important still, for what they impart about his personality and attitudes. In short, Forster is a gifted practitioner of the personal essay, the informal sketch, and the impressionistic critique. His occasional pieces and lectures have more than transient worth, as they form the matrix of *Aspects of the Novel* (1927), *Abinger Harvest* (1936), and *Two Cheers for Democracy* (1951), books which invite us to browse for enjoyment and stimulus.

The familiar essayist's artistry, the intellectual's cultivation, the shrewd observer's penetration into the motives and the personalities of his fellowmen, the poet's sensitivity to place, and the eclectic critic's identification with the achievements of another—such are the leading aspects of Forster's nonfiction. In the late 1920s and thereafter Forster wrote lucid and attractive works, less brilliant than the novels but possessing substantial worth. His toughness of spirit and his consciousness that his standards were important for him lend unity, weight, and even urgency to these books.

"At a Slight Angle to the Universe": History, Travel, and Biography

As a volunteer with the Red Cross in Alexandria during World War I, Forster was impressed, he says in *Alexandria*, by "the magic and the antiquity and the complexity of the city, and determined to write about her" (xv). In *Alexandria* (1922) and in *Pharos and Pharillon* (1923) he considered the city and its denizens of the past and present.[1] In addition to the spell of tradition, colorful places and powerful personalities impart flavor to these books. Forster's aim throughout was to capture both the outlines and the essence of the city: "Immortal, yet somehow or other unsatisfactory, Menelaus accordingly leads the Alexandrian pageant with solid tread; cotton-brokers conclude it: the intermediate space is thronged with phantoms, noiseless, insubstantial, innumerable, but not without interest for the historian" (*Pharos*, 99). Pharos, the great lighthouse that stood for centuries at the mouth of the Nile, brought to focus Forster's reflections upon the older metropolis and its leaders such as Alexander, Philo, Clement, Saint Athanasius, and Arius. He uses the designation "Pharos" to collect his writings on these aspects of Alexandrian history and culture.

More recent activities and people he presented in *Pharos and Pharillon* under the rubric "Pharillon," the "obscure" and smaller successor to Pharos. He appreciated such rich personalities as the seventeenth-century traveler Eliza Fay and the recent poet Cavafy; he depicted vividly such varied aspects of city life as cotton trading and drug addiction; and he related the topography of the present city to the old thoroughfares, the ancient Gates of Sun and Moon, Lake Mareotis, and the surrounding desert. In the first section of *Alexandria* he sketched the history of the city and its culture even more completely than he did in *Pharos and Pharillon.*

Forster's sensitivity, luminous mind, and individual way of seeing things as he stands "at a slight angle to the universe" (*Pharos*, 92) blend to make his Egypt authentic. While neither book is definitive history, each still has literary and stylistic distinction. Thus Forster interpreted with wit and penetration the humanizing influence of Alexandria as she discouraged the ascetic excesses of the early Christians: she taught that "the graciousness of Greece [is] not quite incompatible with the Grace of God" (*Pharos*, 42). With like precision he expressed the difference between Athanasius and the less worldly Arius: Athanasius like Arius "knew what truth is, but, being a politician, he knew how truth can best be enforced" (*Pharos*, 48). In the same wise and witty manner Forster then mocked Neoplatonic spirituality by depicting Plotinus as a soldier, in a campaign against Persia, being "very nearly relieved of the disgrace of having a body" (*Alexandria*, 69).

In many of the writings gathered into *Abinger Harvest* and *Two Cheers for Democracy* [2] Forster followed the course he had pursued in the Alexandria books. Arresting personalities of a later date fascinated him as the Alexandrians of history had, men such as Cardan (Girolamo Cardano), Gemistus Pletho, Voltaire, Edward Gibbon, Samuel Taylor Coleridge, Wilfred Blunt, the Emperor Babur. Each of the portraits reaches beyond known fact to establish the essence of a personality as Forster saw it. The novelist's sense of idiosyncrasy and exact motive, the pungent generalization, the sympathy revealed for the varieties of personality, and the fixing of the man's relationship to the larger world—all contribute to the excitement and creative force implicit in these sketches.

People close to him by blood, his maternal ancestors in particular, preoccupied him. He wrote accurately and affectionately of these forebears in his biography, *Marianne Thornton*, the relative who touched him nearest. Affection tempered his knowledge of their defects, and respect for their virtues compensated for his candid scrutiny of their lives. He evoked the old house, Battersea Rise, not only as a bastion of privilege but as the center for a spacious mode of life and as the symbol for the Thornton steadfastness and seriousness. He appreciated Henry Thornton, the founder of the clan, for his self-sufficiency, despite his Thornton tendency to rationalize his motives by imposing on them a Christian gloss.

Forster manifested the same firmness and sympathy when he came to the next generation and depicted for us the younger Henry and his sister Marianne, and when he traced the proliferation of the family into the later century. The subsidiary family members he brought alive with a kindred force, homage, and humor. For his total picture he gained authority by amply quoting from Marianne's letters and related documents. Aunt Marianne emerges from the past with the same tautness, the same remoteness and charm, that we associate with a figure in a sampler. Forster presented some other views of his Clapham ancestral past in "Mrs. Hannah More" and "Battersea Rise" in *Abinger Harvest* and "Bishop Jebb's Book" and "Henry Thornton" in *Two Cheers for Democracy*.

Forster also wrote of people he had known intimately but who had died. Apparently, he wished to give some lasting form to his impressions of them. His most extensive commemorative work is *Goldsworthy Lowes Dickinson*. When Forster wrote of the years just gone, persons and places tended to merge, so that in *Goldsworthy Lowes Dickinson* turn-of-the-century Cambridge is hardly to be dissociated from the people, especially Dickinson and Nathaniel Wedd, who had meant most to him there. This feeling for place and this evocation of the recent past (the World War I milieu, especially, in which Dickinson achieved some authority with his concept of a League of Nations) endow with immediacy a personality unexciting except to those who knew him well. For what it reveals about Forster more than for what it says about Dickinson, the book is indispensable. The commemorative impulse also led to incidental studies of "Roger Fry," "Forrest Reid," "Howard Overing Sturgis," and "T. E. Lawrence" in *Abinger Harvest* and of "Edward Carpenter" and "Webb and Webb" in *Two Cheers for Democracy*.

Just as in his fiction Forster captured the savor and complexity of a whole civilization—English, Italian, or Indian—so he did in some of his best incidental prose. Preeminent are his writings on India: *The Hill of Devi* and some of the essays in *Abinger Harvest*. Forster's life in India and his immediate reactions to it comprise *The Hill of Devi*. As in *A Passage to India*, Forster communicated a sense of a sprawling continent bursting with life but baffling to our comprehension. His grasp of the involutions of character enabled him to re-create forcibly such dignitaries, British and Indian, as Sir Malcolm Darling (tutor to the Bapu Sahib), Josie (his warm-hearted wife), Colonel Wilson (the paranoid civil servant of the Maharajah who maligned Forster when Forster temporarily took his place), the Maharajah of Chhatarpur, Bapu Sahib (the Maharajah of Dewas Senior), the Dowager Maharini (his contentious aunt), and Scindhia (the Maharajah of Gwalior and the vulgar uncle of Bapu Shaib). Bapu Sahib stands with Forster's other extended portraits of Indians in *A Passage to India*: an all-too-fallible saint, he lingers in the mind with all his contradictions much as do Aziz and Godbole.

For the purpose of creating verisimilitude Forster used copiously his own letters, diaries, and reminiscences in *The Hill of Devi*. But these are not ordinary documents since Forster's talent was such that in all his descriptive prose he appeals subtly to our senses and imagination. He helps us thereby to grasp the full life of an alien civilization, both its surface aspects and its deeper implications. He revealed, moreover, as he did in *A Passage to India*, some of the disparities existing between the culture of the Orient and the British sensibility. He recurred to this contrast between Occident and Orient and the need for mutual understanding in such important essays in *Abinger Harvest* as "Salute to the Orient," "The Mind of the Indian Native State," and "Adrift in India." The India that Forster embraced in novel, autobiography, and travel essay claims our attention principally as a culture important in its own right. Like the writings on India, "Clouds Hill" (T. E. Lawrence's home in Dorset), "London Is a Muddle," "Mount Lebanon" (the Shaker settlement in Massachusetts),

136   E. M. FORSTER

and "Cambridge" (all in *Two Cheers for Democracy*) again
reflect, and gain impressiveness from, Forster's sensitivity to
milieu.

"A World of . . . Richness and Subtlety": Personal, Political, and Social Commentary

Personal, political, and social commentaries are diffused
among Forster's books, and are the principal areas of concern
in his nonfiction. Some of his best essays develop his views on
the relationships that prevail, or ought to prevail, among human beings. The best known, "What I Believe" (*Two Cheers*),
is Forster's fullest statement of his humanism, with its stress on
values personal, intellectual, and tentative in kind. This "con-
fession" gains distinction less from the originality of the ideas
than from the sincerity with which he expressed them. Other
essays from *Two Cheers for Democracy* also weld the personal
and the political. In "Three Anti-Nazi Broadcasts," "The
Menace to Freedom," and "Racial Exercise," Forster evinced
vehement emotion and an uncompromising opposition to intellectual and political tyranny. In one frame of mind, Forster
felt despair almost overwhelm him as he viewed the ap-
proaching cataclysm of war ("Post-Munich" and "They Hold
Their Tongues"). In another, a qualified hopefulness gained
ascendancy ("Tolerance," "The Challenge of Our Time,"
"George Orwell," and "The Tercentenary of the 'Areopagi-
tica' ").

Forster was less involved politically and socially in the earlier *Abinger Harvest*. Characteristically, the social commentary in it centers on English society itself, its distinctive traits,
limitations, and tentative virtues. "Notes on the English Character," with its exposition of middle-class strengths and
hypocrisies, is analytical and, in direction, negative: the deficiencies in the English character predominate over the merits
that we can find in it. All too often Englishmen go forth from
public school "into a world of whose richness and subtlety
they have no conception" (5). In contrast, "Liberty in England" (1935) notes that, for all its defects, English civilization
has always been the guardian of liberty. Satire predominates in

"Mrs. Grundy at the Parkers' " (which exposes British moral hypocrisy); "Me, Them and You" (which excoriates public indifference to the sacrifices made by soldiers in the war); and "The Birth of an Empire" (which lightly scrutinizes British imperialism).

Some of the best essays in *Abinger Harvest* approach modern life from the point of view of the detached moralist: "My Wood" distinguishes an acceptable materialism and carnality from an unacceptable, and "Our Diversions" analyzes the positive and negative aspects of popular culture. Always Forster is persuasive as a social commentator because he was urbane and reserved, yet personal and intelligent.

"Applying Logic to the Illogical": Literary Criticism

Of greater importance than these commentaries are Forster's essays on literature and writers. Apparently, he came to theory and aesthetics late. A few early efforts in *Abinger Harvest* reveal incidental concern with literary theory; and "Anonymity: an Enquiry" dates from 1925, although it is collected in *Two Cheers for Democracy*. This essay is a persuasive description of the work of art as an entity finally separable from the artist who created it and thus all-important in its own right as deriving from the depths of the unconscious.

Forster's best-known book of literary criticism is *Aspects of the Novel* (1927), one of the standard books on narrative, despite its being somewhat tentative in method and in the conclusions reached. Forster not only provided us with terms of discourse for the novel (he divided his book into "The Story," "People," "The Plot," "Fantasy," "Prophecy," and "Pattern and Rhythm"), but he wrote as one who loved literature. He revealed firmness of mind and depth of sensibility; he understood, moreover, the novelist's practice and the problems associated with creativity.

Forster's views on theory and his specific judgments are alike stimulating. He sees the fundamental tension in the novel as that between "life in time" and "the life by values." The life by values the writer expresses through his temperament. As the revelation, then, of the author's view of the world, the novel is to be differentiated from history which, like the novel, finds chronology to be indispensable. The novelist, more concerned with people as such, penetrates further into their hidden lives than does the historian. With Forster, pattern was less important than energy, even when such energy is less than perfectly articulated. Skilled management of point of view, for example, provides a less authentic life for the novel than "a proper mixture of characters." As for "plot," it seeks the causal connections between events rather than their temporal progression (the province of "story"). Curiosity is gratified by the means of plot, as "the memory of the reader (that dull glow of the mind of which intelligence is the bright advancing edge)" (88) helps shape the book in his mind. Some of Forster's other concepts, especially those found in "Fantasy," "Prophecy," and "Pattern and Rhythm," are provocative and often germinal in effect.

Forster is excellent on individual books and authors. He views Thomas Hardy as a writer "who conceives of his novels from an enormous height" (93); he sees Henry James as a master at envisioning the "second-rate" character ("deficient in sensitiveness, abounding in the wrong sort of worldliness" [157]); he praises George Meredith as one who achieves unerring balance between character and the requirements of plot (the concealment of Letitia Dale's changed attitude in *The Egoist* is a great triumph); and he regards Jane Austen as a major novelist because her "characters are ready for an extended life, for a life which the scheme of her books seldom requires them to lead" (75). He cites "the charmed stagnation" of Laurence Sterne's *Tristram Shandy*, he notes the immensities of space in *War and Peace* and how they generate intensity and mute Tolstoy's pessimism, and he observes in Max Beerbohm's *Zuleika Dobson* the "criticisms of human nature [which] fly through the book, not like arrows but upon the wings of sylphs" (118).

Most of Forster's theorizing came in the 1930s and 1940s. Only late in life, apparently, did Forster make conscious (though not systematic) attempts to formulate the views of art and literature on which he had acted for thirty years or more.

Perhaps he did not systematize his ideas earlier because they are not numerous, strikingly original, or rigidly adhered to. He was primarily a subjective, impressionistic critic who tried to identify with an author rather than one who judged books or approached them through literary history.

Regarding literary art, Forster as critic faces two ways. He distrusted analytic discourse because it comes between literature and the reader, but he valued the intelligence as it clarifies and makes more available a masterwork. The critic's task is endless, he said in *Abinger Harvest*, since it consists of "applying logic to the illogical." [3] Criticism helps the artist only minimally; in great matters, his own discernment alone can serve him. But the sophisticated critic can encourage the reader or spectator to know the world of the senses and to sharpen his reactions to it. Criticism can also help "civilize the community" and expose the fraudulent and pretentious. The conscientious critic reveals sympathy as well as detachment, a ranging imagination, and a wide perspective.

Reflecting the organic view of literature embraced by the Romantics, Forster regarded each creation as a self-contained entity in which whole and part fuse closely. He stressed also the internal coherence that is characteristic of the notable work of art. Order results from the active imagination of the artist who impresses his sensibility on all parts of his creation. The writer must be attentive not only to form but to style, for the smaller as well as the larger components of a work acquire intensity to the degree that his sensibility assimilates them.

Forster, who espoused a paradoxical view of art, viewed it as self-contained even while its influence radiates beyond its demarcated universe. Art is at once aesthetic and ethical in nature and authority, at once individual and social in origin and significance. The greater the artist, the more complete is his response to the complexities of life and the more inclusive his vision. In any case, his work bridges the realm of the mind and the empirically perceived world without. He is a realist to the degree that he uses the outer world as basis for his creations but an antirealist to the extent that he captures the symbolical and the transcendent implications in his experience.

In practice Forster combined elucidation of texts and con-

sideration of the artist's general tendencies. Elaborate analysis
of single works is infrequent; but in some of his later critiques
in *Two Cheers for Democracy*—"John Skelton," "George
Crabbe and Peter Grimes," "Virginia Woolf," and "The As-
cent of F-6" (by W. H. Auden)—he concentrated with insight
on individual books or poems. In most of the essays he preferred to consider the writer's canon and to explain its leading
characteristics.

Forster's best critical pieces, though impressionistic in tone
and manner, develop the generalities he derived from examining the corpus of a writer's work. He found, accordingly, that
a "primeval romanticism" explains more about Ibsen's dramas
than any other principle; he saw a horror in T. S. Eliot's earlier
work so intense that the poet cannot always express it clearly;
and he noted in Proust how both curiosity and despair determine the tone and texture of his "epic of decay."[4] In "The
Early Novels of Virginia Woolf," Forster asserted that Virginia Woolf elevates sensation to an aesthetic principle while
she re-creates with immediacy the physical processes of
thought. In "Sinclair Lewis" Forster observed that a realistic
novelist, such as Lewis, might after a while be limited by his
photographic use of detail; in "T. E. Lawrence" he discovered
in the *Seven Pillars of Wisdom* a monumental record not so
much of a great undertaking as of a complex personality; in
"John Skelton" he found a satirist whose bitterness is balanced
by fearlessness; and in "George Crabbe and Peter Grimes" he
saw Crabbe as a large-souled man overcoming his revulsion
from the meanness of East Anglian rural life.

Though Forster developed guiding ideas in examining a
writer, he chiefly conveyed the essential aspects of an author or
an important work through the vivid phrase or succinct statement. His impression, recorded in *Abinger Harvest*, of Septi-
mus Smith in relation to Virginia Woolf's heroine in *Mrs.
Dalloway* is incisive: "His foot has slipped through the gay
surface on which she still stands—that is all the difference
between them" ("The Early Novels of Virginia Woolf," 111).
Then, with Proust's *A Remembrance of Things Past*, Forster
conveyed in *Two Cheers for Democracy* the substance of this
roman fleuve while he memorably epitomized it: ". . . it is full

of echoes, exquisite reminders, intelligent parallels, which delight the attentive reader, and at the end, and not until the end, he realizes that those echoes and parallels occur as it were inside a gigantic cathedral; that the book, which seemed as we read it so rambling, has an architectural unity and pre-ordained form" ("Our Second Greatest Novel?" 224).

Forster and the Art of the Novel: The Novelist's "Creative Finger"

Critics have often censured Forster for the plots of his novels, for an excess of contrivance, an overuse of surprise, and a resort to melodrama. Others have felt that the direction of the action is arbitrary and that the characters are not free to develop normally. Such judgments stem from standards ordinarily applied to realistic fiction, standards that are appropriate in part to Forster's, since social comedy and moral speculation are some of its major components. But these standards are ultimately misleading, as we have seen, since Forster's fiction is romance as well as realism, comprising symbolic drama as well as social observation. Forster was a Moorean realist, but he also desired to reach the inner essence of his experiences. He used plot, therefore, to achieve effects other than the establishing of verisimilitude. He defined his own method best perhaps in defining Virginia Woolf's: "Required like most writers to choose between the surface and the depths as the basis of her operations, she chooses the surface and then burrows in as far as she can" (*Abinger Harvest*, 111).

Ultimately, he wished to communicate his subjective and ecstatic vision of reality, the result in large part of his intense Romanticism of temper. The emotional and transcendent impact of what he created was for him more arresting than its analytic implications. Thus, the facts of perception and the motives underlying action pale before his compulsion to relate them to his intuitive and mystical insights. This realm of the extrasensory overlies the rendition of the social milieu that Forster knew as insider and is intricately intertwined with it; but as it reflects an eternal order of value, this extrasensory

realm is independent of such a milieu. The well-known critic,
F. R. Leavis, who was unsympathetic to this side of Forster,
nevertheless perceived why he rejected the realistic as basis for
any final truth. Forster, Leavis said, was preoccupied with
vitality to the extent that he inevitably was carried beyond
social comedy.[5]

In the tradition of romance with its archetypal figures Forster's books contain major characters that are often more
arresting as felt presences than for the social relationships they
exemplify. These figures become heightened or foreshortened
as they help articulate Forster's vision; and they become symbols as they dramatize his intuitive realizations. On occasion,
Forster designedly sacrificed probability of motive in the interests of ulterior truth. Characters like Gino Carella, Stephen
Wonham, and Ruth Wilcox lack sufficient substance as real
people to be entirely convincing, yet as presences they are not
the aesthetic failures that some critics have declared them to be.
What each lacks for our complete suspension of disbelief is not
added consistency in motivation, but a completer conception
on Forster's part of each personage and his role in the given
book.

As fabulist, romancer, and prophet, Forster evolved complex plots which are, nevertheless, consistent within themselves and which communicate his intuitions more forcibly
than would actions of greater moment and probability. The
alternation of the idyllic and the violent, for example, establishes more vividly Forster's sense of the disjunctions in experience than would a more customary recounting of events.
Such disjunctions achieve, moreover, some resolutions in a
timeless entity extending beyond our ordinary lives in time,
since Forster, as we have seen, was a mediator of extremes and
something of a mystic as well.

Forster once declared in an already cited interview with
Angus Wilson that theme in part determined the incidents.
These are truly important, then, as they relate to theme; as they
illustrate the inner tensions of the characters, their relationships to each other, and their aspirations; and as they
embody the symbolic implications of the fable. Characters,
insofar as they embody theme, must in some part have also

antedated story line as Forster shaped his fiction; and, like the incidents of the plot, they readily attain general, symbolic dimensions.

Forster's characters, then, are often less significant in themselves than for what they suggest as we review the narratives. Except for the "flat" characters—such as most of the Indians and Anglo-Indians in *A Passage to India*, Mrs. Lewin in *The Longest Journey*, and Mrs. Munt and Frieda Mosebach in *Howards End*—the characters have an allegorical aspect which varies in complexity from the crass philistinism of Paul Wilcox in *Howards End* to the complicated humanism and transcendental sensitivity of Margaret Schlegel. His best creations— Lucy Honeychurch, Cecil Vyse, George Emerson, Charlotte Bartlett, Philip Herriton, Caroline Abbott, Gino Carella, Rickie Elliot, Stewart Ansell, Stephen Wonham, Mrs. Failing, the Schlegel sisters, Henry Wilcox, Leonard Bast, Maurice Hall, Alec Scudder, Aziz, Mrs. Moore, Adela Quested, Fielding, and Godbole—are not only significant as recognizable human beings facing recognizable human difficulties but as participants in panoramic dramas of total human concern. They are all actors in spiritual crises and must choose between good and evil, the human and the inhuman, though the act of choice is often perilous for them and disastrous if they choose wrongly. They achieve illumination through risk and even through active suffering; and sometimes the path to transcendence or to salvation is difficult for them to discern or to follow unfalteringly.

More than the characters, some of the incidents—and even the objects—of Forster's fiction gather a symbolic, often a supernal, aura as they bring to focus the ineffable truths that Forster wished to communicate. Incidents and objects become more compelling for what they imply in the full design of the work than for what they literally signify. The dynamic quality of Forster's symbolism depends more on the fact that his characters and actions simultaneously face toward the actual and the ineffable than on the repetition of images and the heightening of style. Forster does not always achieve the fusion of social reality and transcendental value for which he strives, but the fusion is more adroit and the symbolism more organic to total structure than critics like F. R. Leavis and Virginia Woolf admitted. [6]

But, if artistry is not solely a function of Forster's use of rhythm (in the sense of repeated phrases and images) and the presence of a luminous and evocative style, these elements are still integral to his achievement. In *A Passage to India*, for example, such images as the "fists and fingers" of the Marabar Hills, the receding arches in mosque and sky, and the natural phenomena such as stone, fire, rain, and the parched earth all help generate the book's density. The world out there never ceases to be minimally real, however intense the drama within may become or however piercing the moment of visionary ecstasy. And it is the style that gives Forster's fiction—and his nonfiction—its freshness, individuality, and resonance. Almost any page illustrates the beauty and originality of the style but this passage, depicting Leonard Bast and his journey from London to Howards End, is typical:

Tunnels followed, and after each the sky grew bluer, and from the embankment at Finsbury Park he had his first sight of the sun. It rolled along behind the eastern smokes—a wheel, whose fellow was the descending moon—and as yet it seemed the servant of the blue sky, not its lord. He dozed again. Over Tewin Water it was day. To the left fell the shadow of the embankment and its arches; to the right Leonard saw up into the Tewin Woods and towards the church, with its wild legend of immortality. Six forest trees—that is a fact—grow out of one of the graves in Tewin churchyard. The grave's occu-pant—that is the legend—is an atheist, who declared that if God existed, six forest trees would grow out of her grave. These things in Hertfordshire; and further afield lay the house of a hermit—Mrs. Wilcox had known him—who barred himself up, and wrote prophe-cies, and gave all he had to the poor. While, powdered in between, were the villas of business men, who saw life more steadily, though with the steadiness of the half-closed eye. Over all the sun was streaming, to all the birds were singing, to all the primroses were yellow, and the speedwell blue, and the country, however they interpreted her, was uttering her cry of "now." She did not free Leonard yet, and the knife plunged deeper into his heart as the train drew up at Hilton. But remorse had become beautiful. (*Howards End*, 322–23)

We may note, first, the element of the specific—the fact that Forster is describing an actual countryside where places have actual names. He evokes sun, sky, and flowers to the senses, and thereby gains credence for the touch of fantasy surrounding Tewin Church. He not only modulates from concreteness to fantasy but from Leonard's point of view to the omniscient author's. Scene and individual interact as Leonard, in spite of his depression, is at last able to appreciate the beauties of the countryside. One aspect of Forster's deftness is just this ability to objectify the thoughts of an individual by relating them to the people and objects about him. Through indirection but always concretely, Forster is able to convey, furthermore, the evanescent, intangible aspects of personality and the individual's inner life.

Sensitivity to light and shadow accounts in part for Forster's luminous prose. The reactions to physical impressions are so heightened that he conveys through their means an impression that the physical and spiritual are parts of each other, that the streaming lights of nature and the visionary gleams in the soul share reality as parts of a divine entity which we can only intermittently apprehend. In a passage such as the one just quoted, exact observation, supple sensibility, imaginative power, and spiritual exaltation blend to create an authentic poetry in prose.

But the passage reveals intellectual rigor and a subtle mind. There is incisiveness and astringency when the narrator (or Forster), mentioning the rural villas, scorns their businessmen owners as seeing life "with the steadiness of the half-closed eye." Most of the author comment comes in such controlled form, and it elucidates rather than interrupts action and psychology. As Forster regulates tone in observations of this kind, he is able to present matters of portent from a detached, ironic perspective, and to suggest, through oblique means, intuitions more profound than he could have achieved through unmodulated comment. The irony and understatement, the pointed observation and the restrained expression, combine to make the ideas functional rather than intrusive. The aphorisms actually move the novel forward and elucidate character, incident, and value; and they are organic to the novel's life and structure.

Through statement, style, sensibility, and an active imagination, Forster's own personality and values suffuse his fiction. He approximated, in short, his own conception, expressed in *Aspects of the Novel*, of the perfect novelist as one "who touches all his material directly, who seems to pass the creative finger down every sentence and into every word" (72). Such a novelist's work becomes then a manifestation of his own geniality and passion, a reflection of his own lucid intelligence and his visionary intensity.

"This Contradictory and Disquieting World"

Ultimately, the essence of life eludes definition to Forster; and its circumstances are often unpredictable. Since it is in some degree haphazard and chaotic, it cannot devolve in purely ordered patterns. In Forster's world, as one critic says,[7] men do not know enough to control natural, let alone moral, evil, even though Forster conceived the humanist's responsibility to be that of utilizing reason to secure the greatest degree of internal and external order. In Forster's universe, as in Hardy's, coincidence predominates; and sudden, seemingly unmotivated deaths are more frequent than in real life. These deaths thus symbolize the intrusion of the unpredictable into our regulated existences.

Life is not only irrational and unpredictable, but it resists our attempts to define it with precision. It is replete with ambiguities, the ramifications of which are difficult to trace with sureness. In fact, one measure of an individual's insight and understanding is just this knowledge (such as Desmond MacCarthy possessed)[8] of the contradictions underlying the simplest statements. In commenting on William Golding's terrifying vision in *Lord of the Flies*, Forster saw it as facing two ways, toward horror and toward beauty.[9] A. E. Housman was another writer whose work illustrates the major incongruities underlying experience even if he did not always recognize them or satisfactorily resolve them: he denied God at the same time that he denounced Him; he praised both virtue and license; he cherished the phantasmal while he "was incapable of illusions;" he was convinced of treachery everywhere while he dreamed of affection; his manner is "scholarly and churchified," while his matter is "blood-hot or death-cold." [10]

Those writers, according to Forster, are the wisest who acknowledge the strength of such contrary impulsions. Thus George Orwell followed the implications of his experience whether they took him to the "unseen" or around the corner. He wished to learn, in any event, as much as possible of "this contradictory and disquieting world" ("George Orwell," *Two Cheers*, 63). And André Gide was always aware of the involutions and convolutions of the moral life, "the delight, the difficulty, the duty of registering that complexity and of conveying it" ("Gide's Death," 232).

Forster was skeptical of science and its results, especially when the intelligence acts and is oblivious to ethical considerations. Yet his own intelligence allowed him to supplement the fervor of his humanistic philosophy with more rigorous attitudes and concepts. His was no blind faith in human possibilities, no unconsidered belief in the nobility of man's nature and the rightness of all his impulses. Balancing Forster's Romantic enthusiasms, there is his consciousness of man's limitations. If he protested in 1955 against those modern thinkers who emphasize original sin and thereby undermine the humanistic view of life, he was in sympathy in 1962 with the somber view of human nature dramatized by William Golding in *Lord of the Flies*.[11] In that novel, Piggy, the repository of intelligence, is defeated; but he is nevertheless to be admired for his estimate of the forces raised against him and for his efforts to live by the light of his mind.

Golding presents in parable form, Forster observed, the fall of man who, under certain circumstances, relapses from rationality to bestiality. Forster seemingly came to acknowledge that darkness, as well as light, dwells in man's soul and that man is predisposed toward evil as well as good. Forster knew before World War II, moreover, that it was possible to sin, as Lady Macbeth did, "through the depths of her own soul." Like many other human beings, she did not need to encounter the witches to know evil and to have it regulate her actions.[12] The possibilities of such degradation arising from within man's own nature, not the threat from without of alien ideologies, became, for the Forster of the 1930s, the primary menace to civilization. He also appreciated in *Aspects of the Novel* the truth of Melville's dramatization of evil in *Moby Dick* and *Billy Budd* (140–43) and how Melville had to introduce the concept of original sin to right the metaphysical balance of the world he knew.

Forster's consciousness of the presence of evil forces in human nature and in society informs the confessional, "What I Believe." Tolerance, good temper, sympathy—the humanistic virtues—are all precious attributes; but unfortunately, Forster said, they are not widely effective in a world characterized by religious and racial persecution, in which ignorance rules and in which science has been deflected from altruistic ends. Still, in a world of violence, personal relationships, if they are not powerful, provide evidence that values other than empirically perceived ones exist and that men have noble impulses as well as insidious instincts. We can believe still in the residual goodness of human nature; we can, with respect to human possibilities, still "shelter a flickering flame."[13] Forster concluded that earthly life is not a failure but a tragedy, principally because it is difficult to translate private decencies into public ones.

His personality and values are positive in their implications despite his realization of human imperfections and the tragedy of unfulfilled aspirations. In 1951 Forster could say that "human life is still active, still carrying about with it unexplored riches and unused methods of release" (*Two Cheers*, xii). It is just this sense of the inexhaustible nature of human powers that gives his pages their reach and spiritual abundance.

The acute intellect and mature sensibility that we find in Forster he himself finds in Ibsen, "the romantic." The interpenetrations between the solid world of society and the intangible realm of spirit provide focus for Ibsen's art, just as they characterize Forster's own. Both men worked inward to the essence of their perceptions and to a realization of the unexpected relationships among apparently unrelated phenomena provided by these perceptions. What Forster observed of Ibsen's art in *Abinger Harvest* applies as surely to his own:

To his impassioned vision dead and damaged things, however contemptible socially, dwell for ever in the land of romance, and this is the secret of his so-called symbolism; a connection is found between objects that lead different types of existence; they reinforce one another and each lives more intensely than before. Consequently his stage throbs with a mysteriousness for which no obvious preparation has been made, with beckonings, tremblings, sudden compressions of the air, and his characters as they wrangle among the oval tables and stoves are watched by an unseen power which slips between their words. ("Ibsen the Romantic," *Abinger Harvest*, 86)

In Ibsen there is, besides, the fine balance between feeling and detachment that Forster found remarkable in Wilfred Blunt, for instance, and that he himself exemplifies.

In his novels and miscellaneous books alike, Forster's aim was to shape refractory experience to the requirements of order and pattern, but not at the expense of its vitality or the intensity of his vision. He achieved harmony and shapeliness in his fiction, qualities he suspected, however, in writers like Henry James and André Gide who sought too avidly for satisfaction in technique and structure. Still, his own work emanated from that residual sensitivity to aesthetic forms and impressions that the truly creative novelist, according to Forster, must possess. In a general discussion in *Aspects of the Novel* he asserted that such sensitivity results in a beauty which we as readers find amply revealed in Forster's own works, that "beauty at which a novelist should never aim, though he fails if he does not achieve it" (88). He had, moreover, the faith, possessed by the Romantics, in the transforming aspects of the imagination, "the immortal God which should assume flesh for the redemption of mortal passion" ("Anonymity," *Two Cheers*, 88). The creative imagination breathes through all his work and gives it incandescence, whatever its flaws may be.

If Forster lacks breadth, he is always fresh, personal, and original—often profound and deeply moving. A fascination exerted by characters who grip our minds; a wit and beauty

present in an always limpid style; a passionate involvement
with life in all its variety; a view of existence alive to its comic
incongruities and to its tragic implications; and a steady adher-
ence to humanistic values which compel admiration even if
their entire relevance may sometimes be in question—such are
the leading aspects of Forster's work that continually lure us to
it.

As the recent interest in his work signifies, modern readers
have affirmed their conviction of Forster's absolute worth as
critical intelligence and creative artist. The sense of something
uniquely human that is too precious to be lost and that, against
all odds, must be preserved—the conveying of this conviction
in his fiction and nonfiction is the secret of his ongoing appeal
to the intellectual and the general reader alike. It is the steel in
Forster's temperament, not the charm, that finally counts.

Notes and References

Full information about the most available American reprint of Forster's principal works is given below, either when first mentioned in the text or when the book is used as the basis for extended discussion. In a few instances in quoted passages, the standard Abinger Edition text has been used to correct, in minor matters, the text from the reprint used.

Chapter One

1. The authorized life is Furbank's; Francis King's book is also fresh and helpful. Crews, Stone, and Colmer in their books give illuminating accounts of Forster's intellectual life. Many of Forster's miscellaneous books (*Abinger Harvest, Two Cheers for Democracy, The Hill of Devi*, and *Marianne Thornton*) contain much biographical information.
2. "Dante," *Working Men's College Journal* 10 (April 1908): 302; in *"Albergo Empedocle,"* p. 162.
3. Harvey Breit, *The Writer Observed* (Cleveland: World, 1956), p. 55.
4. "Equality," *Mixed Essays* (1879); reprinted in Lionel Trilling, ed., *The Portable Matthew Arnold* (New York: Viking Press, 1949).
5. *Goldsworthy Lowes Dickinson* (New York: Harcourt, Brace, 1934), p. 120. Page numbers in parentheses refer to this edition.
6. For Bloomsbury see the books by Quentin Bell and S.P. Rosenbaum. See also Leonard Woolf, *Sowing* (New York: Harcourt, Brace and World, 1960) and his other autobiographies, and Michael Holroyd, *Lytton Strachey*, 2 vols. (New York: Holt, Rinehart and Winston, 1968).
7. *Sowing*, pp. 162–70.
8. *Bloomsbury: A House of Lions* (New York: Lippincott, 1979).
9. *Goldsworthy Lowes Dickinson*, p. 115.
10. *The Longest Journey*, p. 226.
11. See Forster's "Note on *Arctic Summer*," *Arctic Summer and Other Fiction*, Abinger Edition, pp. 160–162 and "Editor's

Introduction." The versions of this unfinished novel are printed in this volume, pp. 120–215.

12. See "Terminal Note," *Maurice* (New American Library), p. 249.

13. "Notes for a Reply," *Julian Bell, Essays, Poems, and Letters*, ed. Quentin Bell (London: Hogarth Press, 1938), p. 391.

14. New York: Simon and Schuster, 1961, pp. 175-76, 162.

15. See Furbank, 2:200–2, 263–68.

16. Frederick P. W. McDowell, "Introduction," *E. M. Forster: An Annotated Bibliography of Writings about Him*, p. 10.

17. Letters, signed jointly with others, to *Times*, March 13, 1961, p. 15 and January 2, 1962, p. 9; to *Spectator* 209 (November 30, 1962): 856.

18. "India Again," *Two Cheers for Democracy* (New York: Harcourt, Brace and World [1962], Harvest Books), pp. 319–28.

19. "The Long Run," *New Statesman and Nation*, n. s. 16 (December 10, 1938): 971.

20. Furbank, 2:190.

21. "The Individual and His God," *Listener* 24 (December 5, 1940): 801.

Chapter Two

1. For the difficulties that Forster experienced in writing the novel and the various versions of the text, see *The Lucy Novels* in the Abinger Edition and the introduction to that volume and to the Abinger Edition of *Room*. See also Elizabeth Ellem, "E. M. Forster: The Lucy and New Lucy Novels: Fragments of Early Versions of *A Room with a View*," *Times Literary Supplement*, May 28, 1971, pp. 623–26.

2. *A Room with a View* (New York: Random House, 1961, Vintage Books), p. 39. Page numbers in parentheses refer to this edition.

3. That even the least complicated of Forster's novels possesses mythic overtones, John Lucas in "Wagner and Forster: *Parsifal* and *A Room with a View*," *ELH* 33 (1966): 92–117 demonstrates. Forster's characters can be assimilated to Wagner's: Mr. Emerson and George to Titurel and Amfortas, Mr. Emerson also to Parsifal, Lucy to Kundry, and Miss Bartlett and Mr. Beebe to Klingsor.

4. J. B. Beer, *The Achievement of E. M. Forster*, pp. 55–66, discusses exhaustively images drawn from music and painting as they define Lucy.

5. See Abinger Edition, p. 236.

6. Forster's ineffectual Northumberland Aunt Emily was Forster's model for Charlotte. See Furbank, 1:65.

7. *Anatomy of Criticism* (Princeton: Princeton University Press, 1957), pp. 163–86. The quotation is on p. 169. For discussion of other *mythoi*, see pp. 196–239.

8. George Thomson, *The Fiction of E. M. Forster*, p. 38. I am much indebted to Thomson's pioneering study.

9. Robert Langbaum, *The Modern Spirit: Essays on the Continuity of Nineteenth and Twentieth Century Literature* (New York: Oxford University Press, 1970), pp. 127–46. The Introduction to the Abinger Edition gives the circumstances for the composition of *Angels*. Monteriano is San Gemignano; Philip Herriton is in large part Forster's friend, the musicologist E. J. Dent (with an infusion of Forster himself); and the performance of *Lucia* was based on one that Forster attended before Tetrazzini had become world-famous. The novel developed out of an overheard conversation about an English gentlewoman who married an Italian and was unhappy.

10. *Where Angels Fear to Tread* (New York: Random House, 1958, Vintage Books), p. 32. Page numbers in parentheses refer to this edition.

11. See the Endymion reference on the last page of the novel.

12. K. W. Gransden, *E. M. Forster*, p. 28.

13. " 'My Poultry Are Not Officers,' " *Listener* 22 (October 26, 1939): supp. iii.

14. All of Forster's stories in *The Collected Tales of E. M. Forster* (1948) were published prior to 1920 when "The Story of the Siren" appeared (though it dates from 1904 or earlier). The following from the posthumous *The Life to Come and Other Short Stories* (1972) were written early, between 1903 and 1906: "Ansell," "Albergo Empedocle" (published in *Temple Bar*, 1903), "The Purple Envelope," "The Helping Hand," and "The Rock." See "Introduction" to *The Life to Come*. "The Tomb of Pletone" (which I do not have space to discuss) and "Ralph and Tony" appeared in *Arctic Summer and Other Fiction*, Abinger Edition, 1980.

15. See "Editor's Introduction," *Arctic Summer*, especially pp. ix–x.
16. Forster, "Introduction," Giuseppi di Lampedusa, *Two Stories and a Memory* (New York: Coward-McCann, 1962), p. 15.

Chapter Three

1. See Furbank, 1:118; Forster, "Introduction," *The Longest Journey* (London: Oxford University Press, 1960, World's Classics), p. ix.
2. Furbank, 1:116–17; Colmer, p. 69.
3. "Introduction," *Journey*, World's Classics, pp. ix–x.
4. P. N. Furbank and F. J. H. Haskell, "E. M. Forster," *Writers at Work: The Paris Review Interviews*, edited by Malcolm Cowley (New York: Viking Press, 1958), p. 33.
5. James McConkey, *The Novels of E. M. Forster*, p. 37.
6. *The Longest Journey* (New York: Random House, 1962, Vintage Books), p. 3. Page numbers in parentheses refer to this edition.
7. See S. P. Rosenbaum, "*The Longest Journey*: E. M. Forster's Refutation of Idealism" in *E. M. Forster: A Human Exploration*, ed. G. K. Das and John Beer, pp. 32–54 for the facts about Forster, Moore, and *Journey*.
8. Thomson, pp. 141–44.
9. See McConkey, p. 66.
10. Wilfred Stone, *The Cave and the Mountain: A Study of E. M. Forster*, p. 193.
11. "Ritual Aspects of E. M. Forster's *The Longest Journey*," p. 209.
12. See Thomson, p. 139.
13. See Furbank, 1:64, 125n.
14. See McConkey, p. 107.
15. "Introduction," *Journey*, World's Classics, p. xi.
16. Furbank, 1:77.
17. Thomson, pp. 156–59.
18. "A Conversation with E. M. Forster," p. 56.

Chapter Four

1. See "Rooksnest," Forster's earliest surviving literary work, in Appendix, Abinger Edition, *Howards End*.

2. See "Editor's Introduction," Abinger Edition, for documentation of materials in this paragraph.
3. *Howards End* (New York: Random House, 1954, Vintage Books), p. 103. Page numbers in parentheses refer to this edition.
4. Frederick C. Crews, *E. M. Forster: The Perils of Humanism*, p. 106.
5. "*Howards End*: The Sacred Center," *Man in the Modern Novel*, pp. 34–51.
6. *E. M. Forster*, p. 118.
7. Thomson views Ruth Wilcox as the only archetypal character in *Howards End*; and he regards natural objects as having the true archetypal significance for the novel. One can regard the Schlegel sisters and Leonard Bast as, at least, people who quest for the truth and so as partly archetypal.
8. *The Novels of E. M. Forster*, pp. 107–17.
9. Hoy, "Forster's Metaphysical Novel," and Hall, "Forster's Family Reunions."
10. See Edwin M. Moseley, "A New Correlative for *Howards End*: Demeter and Persephone," *Loch Haven Bulletin*, Series 1, No. 3 (1961); and Forster's "Cnidus" (*Abinger Harvest*, pp. 165–69).
11. For contrasting views, see Alan Wilde, *Art and Order: A Study of E. M. Forster*, p. 118; and Thomas Churchill, "Place and Personality in *Howards End*," *Critique* 5 (1962): 61–73.
12. Frederick R. Karl and Marvin Magalaner, *A Reader's Guide to Great Twentieth Century English Novels* (New York: The Noonday Press, 1959), p. 113.
13. Thomson, p. 177.
14. "*Howards End*," *Forster: A Collection of Critical Essays*, ed. Bradbury, pp. 128–43.
15. E. B. C. Jones, *The English Novelists* (London: Chatto and Windus, 1936, edited by Derek Verschoyle, p. 273. Jones also applies this observation to Stephen Wonham of *The Longest Journey* and to Mrs. Moore of *A Passage to India*.
16. See Rose Macaulay, *The Writings of E. M. Forster*, p. 113 and David Cecil, *Poets and Story Tellers* (New York: Macmillan, 1949), p. 195.
17. Furbank and Haskell, *Writers at Work*, p. 28.
18. "*Howards End* and the Bogey of Progress." *Modern Fiction Studies* 7 (1961): 252.
19. Hoy, 130.

20. See F. R. Leavis, *The Common Pursuit*, p. 269, and J. K. Johnstone, *The Bloomsbury Group* (New York: Noonday Press, 1954), p. 228. Wilde, *Art and Order*, p. 114, best analyzes Margaret's reasons for marrying Henry Wilcox; and R. N. Parkinson's "The Inheritors: or a Single Ticket for Howards End" in *E. M. Forster: A Human Exploration*, eds. Das and Beer, pp. 55–68, defends him, on the whole, convincingly.

Chapter Five

1. "Introduction," *The Life to Come and Other Short Stories*, p. xiv.
2. See "Terminal Note," *Maurice* (New York: New American Library, 1975, Plume Books). Page numbers in parentheses refer to this edition.
3. "Terminal Note," p. 250.
4. Cited in P. N. Furbank, "Introduction," *Maurice* (London: Edward Arnold, 1971), p. viii.
5. See K. Natwar-Singh, ed., *E. M. Forster: A Tribute, passim*.

Chapter Six

1. Scholars have exhaustively studied *Passage*. Accounts which have most influenced me are those by McConkey, White, Allen, Dauner, Woodward, Horowitz, Stone, Thomson, Spencer, Bradbury, and Parry.
2. "Syed Ross Masood," *Two Cheers for Democracy*, p. 292. Oliver Stallybrass in "Editor's Introduction" to the Abinger Edition marshals most of the facts concerning the genesis of *Passage*. See also the books on *Passage* or Forster's India by Levine, Das, Robin Jared Lewis (*E. M. Forster's Passages to India*, New York: Columbia University Press, 1979) and the relevant chapters in Furbank. See also *The Hill of Devi* and the miscellaneous writings on India in *Abinger Harvest*, *Two Cheers for Democracy*, and "*Albergo Empedocle*." See also Forster's "Indian Entries from a Diary," *Harper's Magazine* 224 (February 1962): 46–52, 55–56.
3. "Preface," *The Hill of Devi* (New York: Harcourt, Brace, 1933), p. 8. Page references in parentheses are to this edition.

4. Furbank, *E. M. Forster: A Life*, 1:262; 2:133; Stallybrass, "Editor's Introduction," *A Passage to India*, Abinger Edition, p. xxiv.

5. For the importance of the Alexandrian experience, see G. D. Klingopulos, "E. M. Forster's Sense of History and Cavafy," *Essays in Criticism* 8 (1958): 156–65; Jane Lagoudis Pinchin, *Alexandria Still: Forster, Durrell, and Cavafy*; and John Drew, "A Passage via Alexandria," *E. M. Forster: A Human Exploration*, eds. Das and Beer, pp. 89–101.

6. *A Passage to India* (London, Dent, 1942, Everyman's Library), p. xxi.

7. See *E. M. Forster: A Life*, 2:125–30.

8. *A Passage to India* (New York: Harcourt, Brace, 1958, Harbrace Modern Classics), p. 317. Pagination is identical in Harvest Books ed. [1965]. Page numbers in parentheses refer to either of these editions.

9. *Forster's India* (1977), p. 24.

10. See Das, *passim*, and Jeffrey Meyers, *Fiction and the Colonial Experience* (Totowa: Rowman and Littlefield, 1973), Chapter 2.

11. "Forster's Programme Note to Santha Rama Rau's Dramatized Version," Abinger Edition, p. 328.

12. "The Gods of India" (1914), "*Albergo Empedocle*," p. 221.

13. Forster, "The World Mountain," *Listener* 52 (December 2, 1954): 978.

14. Horowitz, p. 81.

15. "The Age of Misery," "*Albergo Empedocle*," p. 201.

16. Natwar-Singh, *E. M. Forster: A Tribute*, p. xii.

17. "The Blue Boy," *Listener* 22 (1957): 444; "A Great Anglo-Indian" (1915), "*Albergo Empedocle*," p. 213.

18. Forster, "Indian Entries from a Diary," p. 51.

19. All commentators agree that the caves are central to the novel. Pessimistic interpreters of the novel, with whom I disagree (Crews, Wilde, Brower), maintain that the negations embodied in the caves are never neutralized, whereas the critics mentioned in Note 1 all feel that the caves represent only the negative pole of reality, at times an overwhelming aspect of experience but still a partial one.

20. *Aspects of the Novel* (New York: Harcourt, Brace and World [1956], Harvest Books), p. 143. Page references in parentheses refer to this edition.

21. Attempts to identify the caves with evil exclusively or to restrict otherwise their meaning represent oversimplifications: see Glen O. Allen's identifying them with intelligence or rationality.

22. Forster, "The Churning of the Ocean," *Athenaeum* (May 21, 1920), pp. 667–68.

23. Benita Parry in *Delusions and Discoveries*, pp. 286–299, suggests that Mrs. Moore's negative vision in the caves is essentially Jainist, emphasizing pessimism, asceticism, and renunciation. Later she passes beyond Jainist limitations, Parry asserts, to become a redeemer as a Hindu deity.

24. Dauner and Stone regard the caves from this standpoint.

25. *Alexandria: A History and a Guide* (Garden City: Doubleday, 1961, Anchor Books, 1961), p. 71.

26. McConkey, p. 141.

27. Angus Wilson, "A Conversation with E. M. Forster," p. 54.

28. "The Art and Architecture of India," *Listener* 50 (September 10, 1953): 421. The quotation is from the book reviewed, Benjamin Rowland's *The Art and Architecture of India* (London: Penguin, 1953).

29. *The Hill of Devi*, p. 169.

30. "The Gods of India," "*Albergo Empedocle*," p. 222.

31. See Allen who identifies "Mosque" with emotion, "Caves" with intellect, and "Temple" with love. See Stone's discussion of "triads," pp. 311–317.

32. The life of the goddess Vishnu furnishes a pattern for the events chronicled in the book and follows the same "seasonal" organization. See Stone, p. 309n.

33. This statement answers Crews's judgment in *E. M. Forster: The Perils of Humanism*, p. 142, that unity cannot be attained. It can be sporadically experienced, but through disorder rather than through logic and harmony. Hinduism does not so much sacrifice the values of humanism (Crews, p. 150) as go beyond them.

34. Forster, "The Indian Mind" (1914), "*Albergo Empedocle*," p. 207.

35. *Aspects of the Novel*, p. 145.

36. *The Cave and the Mountain*, p. 310.

37. Page 81.

38. Forster, "Pessimism in Literature," *Working Men's College Journal* 10 (January, 1907): 10; also in "*Albergo Empedocle*," p. 137.

39. *The Fiction of E. M. Forster*, p. 226.
40. See Edwin M. Moseley, "Christ as One Avatar: E. M. Forster's *A Passage to India*," *Pseudonyms of Christ in the Modern Novel* (Pittsburgh: University of Pittsburgh Press, 1962), pp. 152–63; Dauner; and Stone, pp. 312–15.

Chapter Seven

1. *Alexandria: A History and a Guide* (Garden City: Doubleday, 1961, Anchor Books); *Pharos and Pharillon* (New York: Alfred A. Knopf, 1962). Page numbers in parentheses refer to these editions.
2. *Abinger Harvest* (New York: Harcourt, Brace and World [1962], Harvest Books) and *Two Cheers for Democracy* (New York: Harcourt, Brace and World [1962], Harvest Books). Page references in parentheses refer to these editions.
3. "Roger Fry: An Obituary Note," p. 40. For an elaboration of Forster's theory of criticism and of literature, see my "E. M. Forster's Conception of the Critic," *Tennessee Studies in Literature* 9 (1965): 93–100, and "E. M. Forster's Theory of Literature," *Criticism* 7 (1966): 19–43.
4. "Ibsen the Romantic," "T. S. Eliot," and "Proust," in *Abinger Harvest*. The other essays cited in this paragraph are also from *Abinger Harvest*, except for "John Skelton" and "George Crabbe and Peter Grimes," which are from *Two Cheers*.
5. *The Common Pursuit*, p. 262.
6. See Bibliography for information concerning these critiques.
7. Hyatt Howe Waggoner, *passim*.
8. Forster, "Affable Hawk," *Spectator* 169 (July 23, 1932): 125.
9. "Introduction," *Lord of the Flies* (New York: Coward-McCann, 1962), p. xi.
10. Forster, "Ancient and Modern," *Listener* 16 (November 11, 1936): 921–22.
11. "A Letter," *Twentieth Century* 157 (February 1955): 99–101; "Introduction," *Lord of the Flies*, pp. xi–xiii.
12. "Ghosts Ancient and Modern," *Spectator* 147 (November 21, 1931): 672.
13. Forster, "The Charm and Strength of Mrs. Gaskell," *Sunday Times*, April 7, 1957, p. 10.

Selected Bibliography

PRIMARY SOURCES

Throughout this section, mainly the first English and American editions are listed. For the most readily available American paperback editions, see notes for individual chapters in Notes and References. For other editions of Forster's works, consult Kirkpatrick's *Bibliography* and apparatus in the Abinger Edition, edited by Oliver Stallybrass until his death in 1978. This edition is published by Edward Arnold and distributed in the United States by Holmes and Meier.

1. Novels

All the novels until 1924 appear in the Uniform Edition (London: Edward Arnold, 1924) and in the Pocket Edition (London: Edward Arnold, 1947).

Where Angels Fear to Tread. Edinburgh and London: William Blackwood, 1905; New York: Alfred A. Knopf, 1922; Abinger Edition, Vol. 1, 1975.

The Longest Journey. Edinburgh and London: William Blackwood, 1907; New York: Alfred A. Knopf, 1922.

A Room with a View. London: Edward Arnold, 1908; New York and London: G. P. Putnam's Sons, 1911; Abinger Edition, Vol. 3, 1977; see also *The Lucy Novels: Early Sketches for "A Room with a View,"* Abinger Edition, Vol. 3A, 1977.

Howards End. London: Edward Arnold, 1910; New York and London: G. P. Putnam's Sons, 1910; Abinger Edition, Vol. 4, 1973; see also *The Manuscripts of "Howards End,"* Abinger Edition, Vol. 4A, 1973.

A Passage to India. London: Edward Arnold, 1924; New York: Harcourt, Brace, 1924; Abinger Edition, Vol. 6, 1978; see also *The Manuscripts of "A Passage to India,"* Abinger Edition, Vol. 6A, 1978.

Maurice. London: Edward Arnold, 1971; New York: W. W. Norton, 1971.

Arctic Summer and Other Fiction. London: Edward Arnold, Abinger Edition, Vol. 6, 1980, edited by Elizabeth Heine.

2. Short Stories
The Celestial Omnibus and Other Stories. London: Sidgwick and Jackson, 1911; New York: Alfred A. Knopf, 1923.
The Eternal Moment and Other Stories. London: Sidgwick and Jackson, 1928; New York: Harcourt, Brace, 1928.
The Collected Tales of E. M. Forster. New York: Alfred A. Knopf, 1947; as *Collected Short Stories of E. M. Forster*; London: Sidgwick and Jackson, 1948.
The Life to Come and Other Stories. London: Edward Arnold, 1972, as Vol. 8 of Abinger Edition; as *The Life to Come and Other Short Stories*, New York: W. W. Norton, 1972.

3. Other Books of Prose
Alexandria: A History and a Guide. Alexandria: Whitehead Morris, 1922; Garden City: Doubleday (Anchor Books), 1961.
Pharos and Pharillon. Richmond, England: Leonard and Virginia Woolf, 1923; New York: Alfred A. Knopf, 1923.
Aspects of the Novel. London: Edward Arnold, 1927; New York: Harcourt, Brace, 1927; as *Aspects of the Novel and Related Writings*, Abinger Edition, Vol. 12, 1974.
Goldsworthy Lowes Dickinson. London: Edward Arnold, 1934; New York: Harcourt, Brace, 1934; as *Goldsworthy Lowes Dickinson and Related Writings*, Abinger Edition, Vol. 13, 1973.
Abinger Harvest. London: Edward Arnold, 1936; New York: Harcourt, Brace, 1936.
England's Pleasant Land, a Pageant Play. London: Hogarth Press, 1940.
Nordic Twilight. London: Macmillan ("Macmillan War Pamphlet"), 1940. Similar to "Three Anti-Nazi Broadcasts," *Two Cheers for Democracy.*
Billy Budd: an Opera in Four Acts. Libretto by E. M. Forster and Eric Crozier, Adapted from the Story by Herman Melville. London and New York: Boosey and Hawkes, 1951; revised, 1962.
Two Cheers for Democracy. London: Edward Arnold, 1951; New York: Harcourt, Brace, 1951; Abinger Edition, Vol. 11, 1972.
The Hill of Devi. London: Edward Arnold, 1953; New York: Harcourt, Brace, 1953.
Marianne Thornton (1797–1887): A Domestic Biography. London: Edward Arnold, 1956; New York: Harcourt, Brace, 1956.
Commonplace Book: E. M. Forster. London: Scolar Press, 1978, limited facsimile edition; trade edition forthcoming.

4. Miscellaneous Writings
(1) Pamphlets and contributions to books. Forster wrote several
    pamphlets which were mostly reprinted in *Two Cheers for
    Democracy*. He also contributed chapters or introductions to
    many books. For all these items, see B. J. Kirkpatrick's *Bib-
    liography*.
(2) Uncollected essays, reviews, and letters in periodicals and news-
    papers. These are numerous and important for understanding
    Forster. He has collected only a portion of them in *Abinger
    Harvest* and *Two Cheers for Democracy*. For a full listing, see
    B. J. Kirkpatrick's *Bibliography*. These writings down to 1915
    have been collected in George H. Thomson, ed., *"Albergo
    Empedocle" and Other Writings by E. M. Forster* (New York:
    Liveright, 1971).

SECONDARY SOURCES

This list is a small sampling. Some other more specialized studies are
given, with full bibliographical information, in Notes and References.

1. Bibliographies
Kirkpatrick, B. J. *A Bibliography of E. M. Forster*. London: Rupert
    Hart-Davis, 1965; 2nd ed., 1968, The Soho Bibliographies,
    XIX. Meticulous bibliography of Forster's collected and uncol-
    lected works. Standard.
McDowell, Frederick P. W., ed. *E. M. Forster: An Annotated Bib-
    liography of Writings about Him*. DeKalb: Northern Illinois
    University Press, 1977, Annotated Secondary Bibliography
    Series. Reasonably complete through 1974; abstracting mostly
    done by editor, who evaluates most of the entries.

2. Books and Parts of Books
Beer, J. B. *The Achievement of E. M. Forster*. London: Chatto and
    Windus, 1962; New York: Barnes and Noble, 1962. Sensitive
    readings of novels, stressing Forster's romantic heritage.
Bell, Quentin. *Bloomsbury*. London: Weidenfeld and Nicolson,
    1968. Excellent discussion of Bloomsbury.

Bradbury, Malcolm, ed. *Forster: A Collection of Critical Essays*
Englewood Cliffs, N.J., Prentice-Hall, 1966, Twentieth Century Views. Good collection of standard essays.

————. *"Howards End"* in *Forster: A Collection of Critical Essays*
cited above, in Chap. 4. On Forster's reconciling of comic mode
and poetic vision.

————. *"Two Passages to India: Forster as Victorian and Modern"*
in *Aspects of E. M. Forster*, edited by Stallybrass, cited below,
pp. 123–42. Stresses Forster's reconciling of the temporal-
historical and the transcendent-mystical.

Brower, Reuben A. "The Twilight of the Double Vision: Symbol
and Irony in *A Passage to India*" in his *The Fields of Light: An
Experiment in Critical Reading*. New York: Oxford University
Press, 1951, pp. 182–98. Standard essay on image patterns in
Passage. Mrs. Moore's disillusion is more effective than the
affirmations made in "Temple."

Brown, E. K. "Expanding Symbols" and "Rhythm in E. M. Forster's *A Passage to India*" in his *Rhythm in the Novel*. Toronto:
University of Toronto Press, 1950, pp. 33–59, 89–115. Standard
account of image patterns.

Colmer, John. *E. M. Forster: The Personal Voice*. London and
Boston: Routledge and Kegan Paul, 1975. Illuminating overview, making use of posthumously published fiction and Forster Archive at King's College.

Cox, C. B. "E. M. Forster's Island" in his *The Free Spirit: A Study of
Liberal Humanism in the Novels of George Eliot, Henry James,
E. M. Forster, Virginia Woolf, Angus Wilson*. London and New
York: Oxford University Press, 1963, pp. 74–102.

Crews, Frederick C. *E. M. Forster: The Perils of Hamanism*. Princeton: Princeton University Press, 1962. An excellent critique
though it overstresses Forster's "pessimism."

Das, G. K. *Forster's India*. London: Macmillan, 1977; Totowa:
Rowman and Littlefield, 1978. Valuable for social, intellectual,
and political background for *Passage*.

Das, G. K., and John Beer, eds. *E. M. Forster: A Human Exploration, Centenary Essays*. London: Macmillan, 1979; New York:
New York University Press, 1979. Contains many essays of
high quality and lasting interest.

Furbank, P. N. *E. M. Forster: A Life*, Vol. 1, *The Growth of a
Novelist, 1870–1914*. London: Secker and Warburg, 1977. Vol.
2, *Polycrates' Ring, 1914–1970, 1978*. As *E. M. Forster: A Life*,
one-vol. ed., New York: Harcourt, Brace, Jovanovich, 1978.

Authorized life; indispensable as source for Forster's life and career as writer.

Furbank, P. N. and F. J. H. Haskell. "E. M. Forster" in *Writers at Work, The Paris Review Interviews*, edited by Malcolm Cowley. New York: Viking Press, 1958, pp. 23–35. Important 1953 interview.

Gardner, Philip. *E. M. Forster*. Harlow, Essex: Longman Group, Writers and Their Work, 1978. Best brief account.

———, ed. *E. M. Forster: The Critical Heritage*. London and Boston: Routledge and Kegan Paul, 1973. Reprints criticism on Forster since 1905 and establishes outlines for his reputation.

Gransden, K. W. *E. M. Forster*. Edinburgh and London: Oliver and Boyd, Writers and Critics, 1962; New York: Grove Press, Evergreen Pilot Books, 1962. Informed survey.

Hall, James. "Forster's Family Reunions" in his *The Tragic Comedians: Seven Modern British Novelists*. Bloomington: Indiana University Press, 1963, pp. 11–30. On *Howards End*; the Schlegels preserve vital tradition.

Hardy, John Edward. "*Howards End*: The Sacred Center" in his *Man in the Modern Novel*. Seattle: University of Washington Press, 1964. Sees novel in both realistic and mythic terms.

Hynes, Samuel. "Forster's Cramp" in his *Edwardian Occasions: Essays on English Writing in the Early Twentieth Century*. New York: Oxford University Press, 1972; London: Routledge and Kegan Paul, 1972, pp. 114–22. Discriminating if harsh essay on Forster's homosexuality.

King, Francis. *E. M. Forster and His World*. London: Thames and Hudson, 1978; New York: Scribner's, 1978. Brief but informed and personal account of Forster's life and career.

Levine, June Perry. *Creation and Criticism: "A Passage to India."* Lincoln: University of Nebraska Press, 1971; London: Chatto and Windus, 1972. Background for *Passage*.

Macaulay, Rose. *The Writings of E. M. Forster*. London: Hogarth Press, 1938; New York: Harcourt, Brace, 1938. Initial full-length study, still valuable for some insights.

McConkey, James. *The Novels of E. M. Forster*. Ithaca: Cornell University Press, 1957. Illuminating close readings.

Natwar-Singh, K., ed. *E. M. Forster: A Tribute. With Selections from His Writings on India*. New York: Harcourt, Brace and World, 1964. Appreciative essays by Indians.

Parry, Benita. *Delusions and Discoveries: Studies on India in the British Imagination 1880–1930*. Berkeley and Los Angeles: University of California Press, 1972. Defines intellectual, social, and literary traditions out of which *A Passage to India* grew. Excellent analysis of *Passage*.

Pinchin, Jane Lagoudis. *Alexandria Still: Forster, Durrell, and Cavafy*. Princeton: Princeton University Press, 1977. Alexandria and Cavafy are crucial for Forster's growth.

Pritchett, V. S. "Mr. Forster's Birthday" in his *The Living Novel and Later Appreciations*. New York: Random House, 1966, pp. 244–50. Forster's spiritual importance for modern age.

Rosenbaum, S. P., ed. *The Bloomsbury Group: A Collection of Memoirs, Commentary and Criticism*. Toronto and Buffalo: University of Toronto Press, 1975. Standard source-book.

Sahni, Shaman. "The Marabar Caves in the Light of Indian Thought" in *Focus on Forster's "A Passage to India,"* edited by V. A. Shahane. Madras and New Delhi: Orient Longman, 1975, pp. 105–14. Authoritative essay on its subject.

Smith, H. A. "Forster's Humanism and the Nineteenth Century" in *Forster: A Collection of Critical Essays*, edited by Bradbury, cited above, pp. 106–16. Describes Forster's "two humanisms": a romantic, intuitive one and a rational, intellectual one.

Spender, Stephen. "Personal Relations and Public Powers" in his *The Creative Element: A Study of Vision, Despair, and Orthodoxy among Some Modern Writers*. London: Hamish Hamilton, 1953. Shrewd analysis of Forster's vital but provisional values.

Stallybrass, Oliver, ed. *Aspects of E. M. Forster: Essays and Recollections Written for His Ninetieth Birthday January 1, 1969*. London: Edward Arnold, 1969; New York: Harcourt, Brace and World, 1969. Interesting and informative essays.

Stone, Wilfred. *The Cave and the Mountain: A Study of E. M. Forster*. Stanford: Stanford University Press, 1966. Compendious book. Psychological approach at times distorts fiction but critique of *A Passage to India* is masterly.

Thomson, George H. *The Fiction of E. M. Forster*. Detroit: Wayne State University Press, 1967. Brilliant study of symbolical and archetypal aspects of Forster's fiction.

Trilling, Lionel. *E. M. Forster*. Norfolk, Conn.: New Directions, 1943; London: Hogarth Press, 1944. Pioneer study; stresses Forster both as liberal humanist and artist.

Wilde, Alan. *Art and Order: A Study of E. M. Forster*. New York: New York University Press, 1964. Perceptive book on Forster's increasing inability to find "order."

3. Articles

Allen, Glen O. "Structure, Symbol, and Theme in *A Passage to India*." *PMLA* 70 (1955): 934–54. Provocative Hindu interpretation of Mrs. Moore's experiences in the Marabar Caves.

Berland, Alwyn. "James and Forster: The Morality of Class." *Cambridge Journal* 6 (1953): 259–80. The "pastoral" *Howards End* compared with James's "civilized" novels.

Burra, Peter. "The Novels of E. M. Forster." *Nineteenth Century and After* 116 (1934): 581–94. Reprinted in Abinger Edition, *A Passage to India*. Early essay stressing complexities of Forster's vision.

Daleski, H. M. "Rhythmic and Symbolic Patterns in *A Passage to India*." *Studies in English Language and Literature* 17 (1966): edited by Alice Shalvi and A. A. Mendelow (Jerusalem: The Hebrew University), 259–79. Provocative essay, emphasizing cyclic patterns in *Passage*.

Dauner, Louise. "What Happened in the Cave? Reflections on *A Passage to India*." *Modern Fiction Studies* 7 (1961): 258–70. An archetypal and mythic interpretation of *Passage*.

Harvey, John. "Imagination and Moral Theme in E. M. Forster's *The Longest Journey*." *Essays in Criticism* 6 (1956): 418–33. Stresses the novel's inadequacies.

Horowitz, Ellin. "The Communal Ritual and the Dying God in E. M. Forster's *A Passage to India*." *Criticism*, 6 (1964): 70–88. Stresses death-and-resurrection patterns in novel.

Hoy, Cyrus. "Forster's Metaphysical Novel." *PMLA* 75 (1960): 126–36. Sensitive reading of *Howards End*.

Leavis, F. R. "E. M. Forster." *Scrutiny* 7 (1938): 185–202. Reprinted in *The Common Pursuit* (New York: George W. Stewart, 1952). Germinal if rigid estimate.

Magnus, John. "Ritual Aspects of E. M. Forster's *The Longest Journey*." *Modern Fiction Studies* 13 (1967): 195–210. Astutely defines ritualistic aspects of the novel.

McDowell, Frederick P. W. " 'The Mild, Intellectual Light': Idea and Theme in *Howards End*." *PMLA* 74 (1959): 453–63. Thematic analysis.

Ransom, John Crowe. "E. M. Forster." *Kenyon Review* 5 (1943): 618–23. Illuminating and appreciative early essay.

Spencer, Michael. "Hinduism in E. M. Forster's *A Passage to India*." *Journal of Asian Studies* 27 (1968): 281–95. Presents positive case for Forster's interest in Hinduism.

Traversi, D. A. "The Novels of E. M. Forster." *Arena* 1 (1937): 28–40; reprinted in Gardner. Stresses Forster's desire to mediate extremes but partial inability to do so.

Waggoner, Hyatt Howe. "Exercises in Perspective: Notes on the Use of Coincidence in the Novels of E. M. Forster." *Chimera* 3 (1945): 3–14; reprinted in Bradbury. Coincidences and deaths in Forster's fiction extend our sense of reality, not violate it.

White, Gertrude M. "*A Passage to India*: Analysis and Revaluation." *PMLA* 69 (1953): 641–57. Stresses dialectical organization of *Passage*.

Wilson, Angus. "A Conversation with E. M. Forster." *Encounter* 9 (November 1957): 52–57. Important interview.

Wilde, Alan. Depths and Surfaces: Dimensions of Forsterian Irony." *English Literature in Transition* 16 (1973): 257–74. Irony yields to acceptance of pleasure in the posthumously printed homosexual stories.

Woodward, A. "The Humanism of E. M. Forster." *Theoria* 20 (June 15, 1963): 17–33. Excellent stylistic and philosophical analysis of *Passage*.

Woolf, Virginia. "The Novels of E. M. Forster." *Atlantic Monthly* 140 (1927): 642–48. Reprinted in her *The Death of the Moth* (New York: Harcourt, Brace, 1942). Severe essay, criticizing Forster for failure to weld realism and symbolism.

Index